India &
Britain

Over four centuries of shared heritage

It having been resolved to follow, as nearly as possible, the plan of the Royal Society at London, of which the King is Patron, it was agreed at the first regular meeting, that the Letter here exhibited should be sent to the Governor General and Council, as the Executive power in the Company's territories; and their answer, which is also subjoined, was received in the course of the next month.

———

To the Honourable WARREN HASTINGS, Esq. *Governor General, President*; EDWARD WHELER, JOHN MACPHERSON, and JOHN STABLES, *Esquires, Members of the Council of Fort William in Bengal.*

HONOURABLE SIR AND GENTLEMEN,

A SOCIETY, of which we are Members, having been instituted for the purpose of inquiring into the History Civil and Natural, the Antiquities, Arts, Sciences, and Literature of *Asia*, we are desirous, that you will honour us with accepting the title of our *Patrons*, and request you to consider this application as a token of the great respect, with which we are,

HONOURABLE SIR AND GENTLEMEN,

Your most obedient and most humble Servants,

JOHN HYDE,	THOMAS LAW,
WILLIAM JONES,	CHARLES WILKINS,
JOHN CARNAC,	JOHN DAVID PATERSON,
DAVID ANDERSON,	CHARLES CHAPMAN,
WILLIAM CHAMBERS,	CHARLES HAMILTON,
FRANCIS GLADWIN,	GEORGE HILARO BARLOW.
JONATHAN DUNCAN,	

Calcutta, January 22, 1784.

THE ANSWER.

GENTLEMEN,

WE very much approve and applaud your endeavours to promote the extension of knowledge by the means, which your local advantages afford you in a degree, perhaps, exceeding those of any part of the *Globe*; and we derive great hopes of your attainment of so important an end from our personal knowledge of the abilities and talents of the Gentlemen, whose names we read in the subscription to your address.

We accept the title you have been desirous of conferring upon us of *Patrons* to your Society, and shall be happy to avail ourselves of any occasion that may occur of contributing to its success.

We are, GENTLEMEN,

Your most obedient humble Servants,

WARREN HASTINGS,
EDWARD WHELER,
JOHN MACPHERSON,
JOHN STABLES.

Mr. HASTINGS therefore appeared, as Governor General, among the Patrons of the new Society; but he seemed, in his private station, as the first liberal promoter of useful knowledge in Bengal, and especially as the great encourager of Persian and Sanscrit literature, to deserve a particular mark of distinction; and he was accordingly requested in a short letter to accept the title of President: it was, indeed, much doubted, whether he would accept any office, the duties of which he could not have leisure to fulfil; but an offer of the honorary title was intended as a tribute of respect, which the occasion seemed to demand, and which could not have been omitted without an appearance of inattention to his distinguished merit. His answer is also annexed.

———

GENTLEMEN,

I AM highly sensible of the honor, which you have been pleased to confer upon me, in nominating me to be the President of your Society, and I hope you will both admit and approve the motives, which impel me to decline it.

From an early conviction of the utility of the institution, it was my anxious wish that I might be, by whatever means, instrumental in promoting the success of it; but not in the mode which you have proposed, which, I fear, would rather prove, if of any effect, an incumbrance on it.

I have not the leisure requisite to discharge the functions of such a station; nor, if I did possess it, would it be consistent with the pride, which every man may be allowed to avow in the pursuit or support of the objects of his personal credit, to accept the first station in a department, in which the superior talents of my immediate followers in it would shine with a lustre, from which mine must suffer much

in

---

in the comparison, and to stand in so conspicuous a point of view the only ineffective member of a body, which is yet in its infancy, and composed of Members with whose abilities I am, and have long been, in the habits of intimate communication, and know them to be all eminently qualified to fill their respective parts in it.

On these grounds I request your permission to decline the offer which you have done me the honor to make to me, and to yield my pretensions to the Gentleman, whose genius planned the institution, and is most capable of conducting it to the attainment of the great and splendid purposes of its formation.

I at the same time earnestly solicit your acceptance of services in any way in which they can be, and I hope that they may be, rendered useful to your Researches.

I have the honor to be,

GENTLEMEN,

Your most obedient and most humble Servant,

Fort William, WARREN HASTINGS.
January 30, 1784.

———

On the receipt of this letter, Sir WILLIAM JONES was nominated President of the Society; and, at their next meeting, he delivered the following discourse.

A DISCOURSE

Extracts from the Journal of the Asiatic Society, *Asiatic Researches; or, Transactions of the Society, Instituted in Bengal for Enquiring into the History and Antiquities, the Arts, Sciences, and Literature of Asia*. First Edition published in 1799. See p.16.

India & Britain

Over four centuries of shared heritage

KUSOOM VADGAMA

For Jeremy,
with best wishes and
special thanks!

Kusoom

Oct 2019

AUSTIN MACAULEY PUBLISHERS™

LONDON • CAMBRIDGE • NEW YORK • SHARJAH

This book is dedicated to the men and women, both Indian and British, who have influenced the course of history and determined the fate of the two nations. In doing so, I honour with affection the memory of my mother and father, freedom fighters, and admirers of the British way of life and education.

Elwyn Blacker, my much missed mentor, is remembered with great respect for his huge contribution to the book, which is as much his as it is mine. It is dedicated to him with appreciation and heartfelt gratitude.

To Jon Wynne-Tyson I extend my grateful thanks for his kind and continuous support for all my Indo-British projects over the years.

Elwyn Blacker.

Jon Wynne-Tyson.

ISBN 9781528902243 (Paperback)
ISBN 9781528956697 (ePub e-book)

www.austinmacauley.com

First published (2019)
Austin Macauley Publishers Ltd
25 Canada Square, Canary Wharf
London E14 5LQ

With reference to historical events mentioned in this book, India includes Pakistan and Bangladesh before partition in 1947.

Contents

The former India Office in London, with the Durbar Court at its centre – now the Foreign and Commonwealth Office – was opened by Prime Minister Benjamin Disraeli, MP, in 1868.

The Durbar Court is a masterpiece of design and beauty, used both as a palace and as a drawing room for the nation. The original plan to have two fountains in the Court was cancelled due to the difficulty of installation. Instead, a marble floor was laid with a design suggesting the flow of water. During World War II, when Nissen huts were erected within the Court, the floor was boarded to protect it from damage. The four sides of the Court have granite columns and piers supporting the arches. Niches around it hold marble busts and statues of senior administrators in British India, (such as Warren Hastings, Governor-General of India, right), which serve as a reminder of British rule in India as well as of the combined history of India and Britain.

The Durbar Court is used for major ceremonial gatherings. The grandest of which was in 1902, when it hosted some of the Coronation celebrations of King Edward VII.

Before 1947 the building housed the Indian Office Library. After partition, the question of dividing the Library came up. It so happened that the respected Indian diplomat, Azim Husain and Manzur Qadir, his opposite number in Pakistan, were brothers-in-law. Over friendly discussions they came to a happy and peaceful compromise and agreed to transfer the entire collection to the British Library. It is now known as the Asia, Pacific and Africa collection.

After a failed attempt in the 1960s to demolish the India Office building, it was protected under Grade I Listed Building status.

Indo-British Heritage Trust

The Indo-British Heritage Trust was founded to celebrate and promote 400 years of shared heritage between India and Britain. The Trust received the personal support of former Prime Minister the RT Hon David Cameron MP as well as the Minister of State with responsibility for the Indian subcontinent, the RT Hon Hugo Swire MP.

The links between the two countries began in 1591 when the first trading boats went to India during the reigns of Akbar the Great in India and Queen Elizabeth I in England. In 1600 the Queen granted the Royal Charter to the newly founded Honourable East India Company to trade with India, and in 1614 King James I appointed Sir Thomas Roe as England's first envoy to India. By a happy coincidence, in the same year, the arrival of a young Indian man to England was officially recorded. These two historic firsts were marked in 2014 with a debate held at the Supreme Court of the United Kingdom. The motion was: *This house believes that the Indian subcontinent benefited more than it lost from the experience of British Colonisation* and was Chaired by Keith Vaz MP. Those who spoke against the motion were William Dalrymple, author and broadcaster; Nick Robinson, author and Head of Climate Change Centre, HSBC; Shashi Tharoor, author and member of Indian Parliament. Those speaking in favour were Nelofar Bakhtyar, Art Editor (*Newsweek Pakistan*) and Lahore Literature Committee member; Martin Bell, former independent member of parliament, BBC journalist and British UNICEF Ambassador and Kwasi Kwarteng MP, author of *Ghosts of Empire* about the legacy of the British Empire. Before the debate the distinguished audience voted in favour. After the debate the motion was defeated by a large majority.

It was on 10 January 1616 that Sir Thomas Roe presented his credentials to the Court of the Moghul Emperor Jahangir, in Ajmer. His mission was to obtain protection for the Honourable East India Company in India. This historic moment marked the official beginning of the relations between India and England. It is magnificently depicted in the mural in St Stephen's Hall in Parliament. Painted by Sir William Rothenstein, it was unveiled by the Prime Minister Stanley Baldwin MP in 1928.

Another historic event of the year 1616 was the baptism of the Indian who had arrived in England in 1614. The ceremony took place at the St Dionis Backchurch in the City of London on 22 December. He was given the name 'Peter' chosen personally by King James I. Among the congregation were the Lord Mayor of London, Privy

Council, City Aldermen and officials of the Honourable East India Company. Not much is known about 'Peter', who returned to India soon after the baptism.

This 400th anniversary was in itself an historic event. That it should also commemorate the centenary of the First World War is significant. More than 1.5 million Indians came to the colours and over 65,000 died for the Allied cause. The first of the 11 Victoria Crosses awarded to Indian soldiers was presented to Khudadad Khan by King George V at Buckingham Palace on 31 October 1914.

Despite the huge differences in culture, religion and language and separated by thousands of miles, the bond between the two countries has continued for over 400 years, from the reign of Queen Elizabeth I to the reign of Queen Elizabeth II.

It has been an honour and a privilege to have the Foreword from Dr Alice Prochaska, Principal, Somerville College, Oxford and Patron of the Indo-British Heritage Trust. Contact with Indian students at her college and visiting India, has given her a personal experience of the relationship between the two countries. Further cementing the special relationship between the two countries, Dr Prochaska has launched a Cornelia Sorabji Post-Graduate Scholarship, named after the noted student who studied at Somerville in 1889. To mark the 150th anniversary of Cornelia Sorabji's birth, on 15 November 2016, she organised a celebratory event at India House, hosted by the Acting High Commissioner His Excellency H E Patnaik. Proud of its connection with India, Somerville has portraits of Cornelia Sorabji presented by the author; Mrs Vijaya Lakshmi Pandit, Indian High Commissioner (1954–61); and Indira Gandhi, Prime Minister of India (1966–77, 1980–84), who was a student there. For that and all her kindness we thank Dr Prochaska most sincerely for her much valued contribution.

Michael Blacker
Kusoom Vadgama
Co-Chair IBHT

400 Years of Indo-British Relations

Dr Alice Prochaska,
Former Principal of Somerville College, Oxford

Millions of living Indo-British inheritances contribute to a swelling tide of shared heritage: always changing and always staying the same, like the 'Ocean of the Stream of Stories' described by Salman Rushdie. This book celebrates many of those inheritances, and there will be new insights in its pages for all of us.

It is to be hoped that policy makers and opinion formers in both countries will continue to welcome each other, in person and in our respective organisations, as we have done throughout the past four hundred years. In the educational sphere alone, there is so much to celebrate: the education of prime ministers from Jawaharlal Nehru and his daughter Indira Gandhi, to Manmohan Singh; and the life-changing experiences of some of India's earliest university-educated women, like the pioneering lawyer Cornelia Sorabji and a long line of influential academics and diplomats. The former Indian High Commissioner in London, Navtej Sarna, picked up on this theme with his recent novel based on the life of Maharaja Duleep Singh, who was feted at the court of Queen Victoria but deprived of his inheritance, and whose daughters studied alongside Cornelia Sorabji at Somerville College, Oxford.

In the arts as well, a fertile cultural exchange has existed from the earliest days. One has only to think of the ubiquitous and much-loved Paisley or Boteh design, with its origins in Persia and its spread from Moghul India in the seventeenth century to Britain where it acquired the name of the Scottish town whose industry depended on it. It remains perhaps the best loved and most widely used motif in the world for textiles, wallpapers and much more. British artists travelled to India from the seventeenth century onwards, sending home their representations of the astonishing landscapes, architecture and people of the land that they found endlessly beguiling. Indian artists, the most celebrated in recent times perhaps being Anish Kapoor, have influenced the fine and decorative arts of Britain for centuries, giving rise now to a rich reciprocal trade.

British and Indian literature also display a fine reciprocity. The names of just a few winners of the Man Booker prize evoke the respect and love felt by the reading British public for some of the great works by Indian contemporary writers: Salman Rushdie, Arundhati Roy, Kiran Desai, Aravind Adiga – not to mention those who surely will appear on that list at some point, like Vikram Seth and Amitav Ghosh. British scholars studied the ancient languages and religions and the history of South

Asia and learned from the scholars they encountered. In their turn, people like the eighteenth-century Sanskrit specialist and founder of the Asiatic Society of Bengal, Sir William Jones, enriched India's own understanding of its origins.

India has supplied also some of the most important territory for social science and scientific investigation by British administrators and academic scientists, from the data-gathering of population scientists, meteorologists and epidemiologists in colonial times, to present-day investigations of climate change and conservation issues. Today, important scientific advances draw on medical and pharmacological collaborations and many others. The research arms of British and Indian businesses depend on talent from the two countries, working together to provide commercial as well as scientific innovations.

Most of these relationships come with their attendant darker histories. Writers including Rudyard Kipling, E M Forster, Paul Scott and William Dalrymple have portrayed, with varying degrees of awareness, the incomprehension, the sense of otherness, the colonial exploitation, the military repression, and accusations of barbarity that characterised so much of the relationship between British and Indian people in the past. What this book demonstrates, however, is that there remains an enormous amount to celebrate, and a deep well of shared heritage on which to draw for the benefit of generations in both Britain and India in the future.

Alice Prochaska

Dr Alice Prochaska, a professional archivist, historian and Principal of Somerville College Oxford (2010–2017).

A Unique Relationship

Zerbanoo Gifford, Founding Director of The Asha Centre

There is no denying the fact that the destinies of Britain and India have been tied up in an inexplicable way. It goes way beyond the common obsession with cricket, or the passion for chicken tikka masala overtaking the British staple of fish and chips.

'It is only when you get to see and realize what India is', announced Lord George Nathaniel Curzon in a speech at Southport, 'that she is the strength and the greatness of England, you feel that every nerve a man may strain, every energy he may put forward, cannot be devoted to a nobler purpose than keeping tight the cords that hold India to ourselves.' Now who would have thought that the words of Lord Curzon, Viceroy of India (1899–1905), would have a startling relevance more than a century later?

Putting those words into perspective was the former Prime Minister David Cameron, who visited India three times while in office. The 'special relationship' which he said Britain and India shared spoke of a new equation in the tale of two countries. It signalled an open interest in establishing a serious relationship with one of the world's fastest growing democracies and, to me, a reversal of investment roles. To understand the subtle shift of power, we need to revisit the passage to India. Let's sail back 400 years to the 1600s, when trade between Tudor England and Mughul India was established.

Though there has always been a steady migration of Asians from all walks of life to Britain, the birth of the British East India Company marked a definite shift in the culture and history of both nations. It played a crucial role in the writing of chapters on imperialism and colonisation of India. Violent and non-violent political uprisings, accompanied by anti-colonial nationalism and the civil disobedience movement, finally saw India gain its independence. However, even after the British left Indian shores, Indians suffered from a colonial hangover for a very long time. It took decades to recover from the days of the Raj.

But recover they did, bringing about a paradigm shift in the balance of power. Over the last few years, there has been much talk about India being a 'superpower' with the benefit of a young population. Seventy per cent of Indians are now under the age of 35, which contributes to a huge knowledge-based economy.

India is the third largest investor in the UK, with at the last count more than 500 Indian companies establishing offices. When the Tata Group, India's biggest vehicle maker, with a squeaky-clean reputation, came up with the requisite cash injection to take over the luxury car makers Jaguar and Land Rover, it saved the jobs of over

15,000 British workers, and enabled these iconic brands to survive in a fiercely competitive market. The world sat up and started taking notice. Other companies like Tetley Tea, and the steel maker Corus, were also acquired by the Tata Group, which is now the largest industrial house in Britain. In the IT sector there were other cross-border acquisitions.

Until recently, the wealthiest man in Britain was an Indian. Lakshmi Mittal, the Indian steel magnate, not only took the top spot in the *Sunday Times* Rich List for eight consecutive years, but also helped Britain's cash-strapped Labour Party out of a financial crisis. On the other hand, in a fresh push for international growth, the very British Marks & Spencer plans to make India its biggest foreign market. Both Marks & Spencer and Tesco, which intends to invest £68 million in India's closely protected retail sector, have set up joint ventures with local companies in India. UK companies announced an investment of £19 billion in India, said to be eighteen times more than any previous year.

All this points to the fact that the relationship between Britain and India has transcended the historical and political matrix. The two countries are now working closely together on issues such as climate change, education and the fight against terrorism, as well as on fostering sporting ties. We have now reached an exciting time in history, when the millennial generation of Indians circling the globe with frequent-flier miles are on an equal footing with their British counterparts. Educated at the best schools and universities abroad, they not only speak English with a perfect British accent but also share the mindset of their British friends. The colonial hangover has slowly been exorcised. To put it simply, it's almost wiped out.

More importantly, nearly 1.5 million people of Indian origin live in Britain. A closer look at the third-generation Indians living in the UK clearly shows them to be a new creative generation who seek to change the world with innovation and public service responsibility. I believe that this young vanguard will herald a refreshing cultural movement. It is this 3-D generation, witness to a global revolution in virtual connectivity, that has a genuinely different take on things, be it in the IT sector, sustainable energy systems, or the IPL (Indian Premier League) matches that took Twenty20 cricket onto a world stage. Generation Xbox is inching towards a more inclusive, global society. The science and technology breakthroughs they come up with benefit not just their two nations but the whole world. The future now rests on all young and equal citizens of a country that is rich in history. It comes, too, with the sweet promise of a legacy the young Indians will leave behind in Great Britain.

Zerbanoo Gifford

The Founding Director of the ASHA Centre, Royal Forest of Dean, Gloucestershire, empowering the young to be leaders of tomorrow. www.asha.org

What they said

Many eminent personalities expressed their views on India and made comments on events and individuals of their time. Among them were those who could not bear to lose the domination of India and those who criticised the unjust rule of the country as well as those who expressed delight at India being liberated from foreign power.

'The loss of India would be final and fatal to us. It could not fail to be a part of a process that would reduce us to the scab of a minor power.'
WINSTON CHURCHILL MP
House of Commons February 1931.

"Animated with all the avarice of age, and all the impetuosity of youth, they roll in one after another, wave after wave, and there is nothing before the eyes of the native but an endless, hopeless prospect of new birds of prey and passage, with appetite constantly for a food that is continually wasting.'
EDMUND BURKE MP
House of Commons about the East India Company, 1783.

'As long as we rule India, we are the greatest power in the world. If we lose it, we shall drop straight away to a third-rate power.'
LORD CURZON
1901

'Never convinced that the British really intended to keep their promise to leave, the Indians are deeply impressed when they actually did and the disappearance of their hostility was almost an overnight phenomenon. I do not think they have forgotten the long years of inferior status, or the economic damage the British inflicted on India, but even though they recognise that some of their present-day ills stem from British rule, their grievances have been swelled up in a surge of genuine friendliness. They tend to remember good things the British did and ignore the bad; and it is a fact that today the British are remarkably popular there'

MRS ELEANOR ROOSEVELT
Comments after Indian Independence, 1947.

'With an elegance and style that will compel and will receive an instinctive response throughout the world, Attlee and Mountbatten have done service to all mankind by showing what statesmen can do, not with force and money but with lucidity, resolution and sincerity.'

WALTER LIPMAN
American Political Commentator, 1947.

'During the centuries that the British and Indians have known one another, the British mode of life, customs, speech and thought have been profoundly influenced by those of India- more profoundly than has been realised.'

LORD MOUNTBATTEN
Eve of Indian Independence Day 14 August 1947

'We welcome India's new and enhanced status in the world community of sovereign independent nations, assure the new Dominion of our continued friendship and goodwill, and reaffirm our confidence that India, dedicated to the cause of peace and to the advancement of all peoples, will take its place at the forefront of the nation's of the world in the struggles to fashion a world society founded in mutual trust and respect.'

HARRY TRUMAN, President of United States of America-
Eve of Indian Independence, 12 August 1947

Introduction

This book celebrates over 400 years of Indo-British shared heritage. The history of that heritage is like no other history of a relationship between two countries. Though totally different in language, culture and religion, and thousands of miles apart, the people of the greatest ancient civilisation of India, and the people of the most powerful trading seafaring nation of all, England, came to be involved with one another. The impact on the political, economic, cultural and scientific – but not religious – lives of the people of these two countries was lasting. Ever since, the history of India has been the history of Britain and of the British Empire; without the story of the Indian contribution to the British way of life, from when the first Indian set foot on British soil, the history of the British Empire is not complete.

Though India had already been conquered in 1526 by the Moghuls before the British first went there in 1591, the conquest by the British was quite different. They changed India's law, language, administration, education and communications. Most importantly, they helped India to discover its past. British scholars deciphered the

Right: Akbar the Great was a brilliant general who expanded the Moghul Empire. He is remembered, along with Emperor Ashoka, as one of the greatest rulers India has ever seen.

Far right: Queen Elizabeth I granted a charter to the East India Company in 1600 to trade with India, which had an unforeseen and lasting effect on the history of the two countries. In granting the Royal Charter, she limited the Company's investors' liabilities, as well as her own, creating the world's first Limited Company.

glory and grandeur of the transcripts of Emperor Ashoka; they translated Buddhist literature and sacred texts of the East, and revealed the knowledge of the ancient saints. They also did work on Sanskrit in general and on *Vedas* in particular. For all this, a debt of gratitude is owed to Indologists like Sir William Jones, Max Müller, A B Keith, John Marshall, Monier Monier-Williams and many others.

But there is also a debit side to the British rule in India. British industry in India systematically drained the country of capital resources. Britain's policy of divide and rule made Hindus and Muslims enemies of each other, leading people like Dadabhai Naoroji to condemn British rule in India as 'un-British', and eventually to the partition of India in 1947 and the emergence of two independent nations, India and Pakistan – later three, with the foundation of Bangladesh. Then there was the Mutiny of 1857 and, worse still, the massacre at Jallianwala Bagh of 1919. Both were acts of unforgivable brutality that will never be erased from the history books.

But when the end of the Raj came, and the British gave up the country they were masters of for nearly 200 years, they left with understandable sadness but also with a great deal of goodwill. There was amicability between the last Viceroy, Lord Louis

Sir William Jones (1746–1794) went to India in 1783 as a Calcutta Supreme Court Judge. A scholar of ancient India and its culture, he learnt Sanskrit and translated the *Vedas* and other ancient scriptures and literature. In 1784 he founded the Asiatic Society, to encourage Oriental studies. It was the first institution of its kind in India. He also launched the journal *Asiatic Researches* which promoted excellence in art and science and an understanding of the ancient history of India.

Warren Hastings, the first de facto Governor-General of India, approved and applauded the Asiatic Society but declined the nomination to be its first President because of the demands of his official duties. Sir William Jones was then nominated President of the Asiatic Society.

Mountbatten, and the first Prime Minster of India, Jawaharlal Nehru: after the flag-hoisting ceremony, the Viceroy drank a toast 'To India', and the new Prime Minister raised his glass 'To King George'.

For all the misdeeds of the British in India during their almost 200 years of Colonisation and over 70 years after independence, there is now a demand for reparations, to reverse the decision made by the Indian National leaders after independence, not to seek revenge in any form. These men and women who were at the receiving end of British injustice and repeatedly imprisoned, showed no bitterness towards the former rulers. To overturn their judgement is nothing short of contempt for their honourable decision. Calls for reparations are as irrelevant as they are impractical and has no place in the Indo-British relationship; the demand for the return of the Koh-i-Noor diamond is misguided because the rightful owner is neither India nor Britain, but the family of the Maharaja Ranjit Singh of Punjab. With no living descendants, the best showcase for it is in the Tower of London, in the Queen Mother's crown, where it should remain to be seen by the world. Even if it stays in Britain for a thousand years it will still be known as the Koh-i-Noor diamond of India.

General Maharaja Sir Ganga Singh of Bikaner (1880–1943) served both in France and Egypt during World War I and was the first Indian Prince to be delegated to the Imperial War Conference and Cabinet. He provided a stream of Indian recruits and gave thousands of pounds to the Imperial Treasury.

The Indo-British connection has left permanent marks, both good and bad, on each country. Would relations continue after independence in 1947, it was often asked – and what of the future? The bonds of friendship, although changed, have indeed strengthened.

There is now a large Indian population that has made Britain its home. For the second- and third-generation Indians, Britain is the only homeland they know. They are loyal citizens, faithful to the monarch and truly and completely part of British society. In law, medicine, finance, politics, education, the armed forces, arts and sport, they are members of the organisation to which they belong, and not a group separated by culture, religion or ethnicity. So why still put them in the category of 'the diaspora?' Such labels which set us apart, are as unacceptable as they are unhelpful, creating a culture of 'them and us'. We are all citizens of Britain.

It is not possible to do justice to every significant event and to each important individual in the 400-year combined history of the two countries. But there are black holes of history on both sides that need to be acknowledged. For Britain, it is a case of recognising the Indian contribution to the British way of life – something which is often bypassed. It is sad as well as inaccurate, for example, to give the impression that Britain won the two world wars single-handedly. At the annual Festival of Remembrance at London's Royal Albert Hall, the sacrifices of Indian soldiers have never been mentioned. The opinions of their families in India are apparently considered not worth reporting. Even in the centenary of the First World War, the names of Lord Sinha and the Maharaja of Bikaner, joint members of the War Cabinet in 1919, remain confined to the library archives.

We need to remind ourselves of the forgotten heroes, even if their achievements may not seem relevant today – names like Raja Ram Mohan Roy, Srinivasa Sastri, Gopal Krishna Gokhale, Vallabhbhai Patel, Jamsetji Tata, Swami Vivekananda, Sir Tej Bahadur Sapru and Keshub Chandra Sen, all of whom made an intellectual, political and moral impact on Britain. The same is true for the artistic and exotic splendour of India enthusiastically displayed during Queen Victoria's reign.

For India, it is a matter of honouring all those who fought in the fight for freedom. Overlooking the work of the pioneers like A O Hume, Gokhale, Tilak, Lajpat Rai, Subhash Chandra Bose, Bhikaji Cama, Savarkar, Shyamaji Krishnavarma, Sardar Patel, Maulana Azad, Sarojini Naidu, Baldev Singh, Sir William Wedderburn and many others, is unforgivable.

In spite of all the ups and downs in the relationship between the two countries, there is a mutual interest in maintaining the bond between their peoples. The obituary of the Indo-British relationship will never be written.

CHAPTER 1
The First Englishmen in India

Below: Sir Thomas Roe was appointed by James I as England's first envoy to the Court of Jahangir in 1614 to bolster the struggling East India Company.

Below right: Sir Thomas Roe's first audience at the court of Jahangir in 1616.

The first recorded Englishman to go to India was Thomas Stephens (1547–1619), a Jesuit priest and a missionary, in 1579. He was also the first Englishman to sail to India via the Cape of Good Hope. Stephens decided to leave England for fear of religious persecution, having converted to Catholicism during the reign of Queen Elizabeth I. Disguised as a servant, he escaped to Rome, where he was given permission to travel to India via Portugal. He landed at Portuguese Goa and settled there, soon learning to read and write the Konkani and Marathi languages, and becoming the first person to compose a Konkani grammar. Also acknowledged in India is his contribution to Goan and Christian literature. Stephens married a local girl, and their children became the first recorded Anglo-Indians. In 1989, as a mark of gratitude for his contribution to the Konkani language, the Thomas Stephens Konkani Kendra (Thomas Stephens Konkani Centre) was founded in Goa, an institute run by the Society of Jesus and dedicated to the study and propagation of the Konkani

language. It is actively involved in historical research and the teaching of Latin, and has a well-maintained and carefully labelled botanical garden.

The first Englishman to establish an Indo-British relationship at the highest official level was Sir Thomas Roe (c.1581–1644), who in 1614 was appointed by King James I to be England's first Envoy to the Court of the Moghul Emperor Jahangir (1605–27), with a mission to arrange a commercial treaty with India and promote the extension of trade in the East with the East India Company, which paid for Roe's expenses. He was also to protect the Company at Surat, 'the cradle of the British Empire', at a time when the well-settled Portuguese in India still treated the English as 'theeves'[sic].

After many delays, Roe finally had an audience at the Moghul Court in 1616. The Emperor refused to treat King James I as an equal but did give Roe a *firman*, a Royal Charter, which promised protection for the resident English merchants in the area controlled by the Moghul Court.

Roe was an eminent diplomat, scholar and patron of learning. His diary of everyday life in India gives a vivid and lively account of his life at the Moghul Court – explaining, for example, how his request not to prostrate himself before the Emperor was accepted by the Court. Instead he just bowed three times and gave the translated letter from King James I to the Emperor. He then presented gifts to the Emperor including an English coach, swords, hats, and alcohol, which was well received – in fact, he and the Emperor became good friends and drinking partners. Roe became an object of interest for the harem, whose inquisitiveness led them to cut holes in the curtain that separated them, to enable them to have a good look at the Englishman.

One feature of Roe's time at the Embassy was the exchange of images of the two countries' rulers. He had brought with him miniature paintings by his cousin Isaac Oliver (c.1565–1617), a leading miniaturist, with which the Emperor was most fascinated, and it is from this time that Moghul and English portraits exhibit a great similarity. Roe wrote that he was 'treated with more favours and onward grace' than ever was shown to any ambassador. In 1605 Roe was knighted by King James I, and in 1614 was elected Member of Parliament.

The irony is not lost in the magnificent mural in the Palace of Westminster depicting the first, defining moment in Indo-British relations: the historic meeting on 10 January 1616 between the Moghul Emperor Jahangir, descendant of the Muslims who conquered India in 1526 at the battle of Panipat, and Sir Thomas Roe, the English forebear of those who ruled India for 90 years after the Mutiny of 1857. The next, arguably more significant, milestone date came in 1947 when, after 421 years of foreign rule, India gained independence and became self-governing.

James I (1566–1625) was keen to establish a strong trading relationship with the Indian court.

CHAPTER 2
The East India Company: The World's Most Powerful Corporation

It all began when, in 1591, the first three trading boats from England went to India in the reign of Queen Elizabeth I of England and of the Moghul Emperor Akbar the Great in India. Captain James Lancaster brought back with him information that gave rise to subsequent commercial voyages to India. This determination of the English to trade with India had come about when the Dutch East India Company, which controlled the spice trade, put up the price of a pound of pepper – 'black gold' – by five shillings. In 1599, the resulting price war led twenty-four merchants in the City of London to found a trading company, and in 1600, Queen Elizabeth granted what was now the English East India Company a Royal Charter, giving the Company the monopoly to trade with India, with renewal of the Charter every twenty years. This was to be the dawn of the British Empire.

In 1608, William Hawkins became the first Englishman to present himself to the Court of the Moghul Emperor Jahangir, who signed an imperial *firman* authorising the English East India Company to set up trading posts in India. The Company assured the locals that they had come to India for 'trade, not territory', and its lucrative deals in spices, gum, sugar, raw silk and muslin cotton were welcomed by the Indians. Hawkins became a great drinking companion of the Emperor, who called him 'English Khan'.

As the Company expanded in India it increasingly influenced local politics – purely for selfish reasons, to safeguard its lucrative business ventures. The early English arrivals to India had all been illegal immigrants who strode arrogantly into the country. As they increased in numbers, so did their influence on the lives, laws and the language of the people. The Company even started interfering with tax, introducing laws to raise revenues. By the end of the seventeenth century, there was a gradual expansion of its chain of factories around the coast of India. As a consequence, law courts and civic corporations came into being, based on the English legal system.

The man who is most credited with building the structure of the British Raj, and securing Britain's authority in India, was Robert Clive, who during his time as

The *Red Dragon* commanded by Captain James Lancaster led the first East India Company voyage in 1601.

Commander-in-Chief of British India won fame and immense fortune. In 1757 it was his defeat of Siraj-ud-Daulah at the Battle of Plassey that truly set the course for the establishment of the British Empire, and the transformation of Britain from a small seafaring country into a great imperial nation. British supremacy in India would be consolidated in the first half of the nineteenth century under Lord Cornwallis, Arthur Wellesley, the Duke of Wellington, and Charles Theophilus Metcalfe, the founding fathers of British India.

In 1784 William Pitt's India Act saw British India jointly governed by the East India Company and the Crown, but by 1818 the Company had come to be recognised as the supreme ruler of India, including by now a military capability with which to rule the provinces – and there was nothing that could be done about its legitimacy. Casualties of this British domination of India included Tipu Sultan, the ruler of Mysore, and the first Indian king to be killed defending his territory against the British East India Company. In 1849, Lord Dalhousie annexed Punjab, removing the ten-year-old Maharaja Duleep Singh, his Koh-i-Noor diamond having been surrendered to Queen Victoria.

East India House in Leadenhall Street in the City of London was built in 1726 and demolished in 1861 after the Mutiny of 1857.

At the same time, others from Britain were working for India's interests. With the help of Raja Ram Mohan Roy the Indian social reformer, Lord William Bentinck, British soldier and statesman and Governor-General of India from 1828–35, took steps to abolish *suttee*, as well as making polygamy and child marriages illegal. It was the initiative taken by William Henry that by the 1870s saw the end of the Thug cult (an organisation of robbers and assassins). The aggressive actions of some British officials cannot be forgiven, but neither can the lawful activities of others, in the interests of the people of India, be forgotten.

From the time when the East India Company made its first trading voyage to India in 1600, until its commercial activities came to an end in 1833, a total of 2,000 ships had been in operation, transporting cargo and passengers between India and England but not without heavy loss of merchandise and human life. No fewer than 200 vessels were shipwrecked. British as well as Indian lives were lost. Many ships had carried gold bullion and ingots, woollen goods, coins, spices, and manufactured items. As well as spices, the British traders also brought back carpets and textiles — indeed, textiles became their main interest: calico, cotton, muslin, and mixed cotton and silk fabrics. Soon the British were exporting raw silk to Europe, and during the 17th and 18th centuries they managed to control the international trade in textiles,

Robert Clive: Awarded the title of Clive of India for his victory in 1757 at Plassey, where he defeated the Nawab of Bengal, laying the foundation of British power in India. The *de facto* founder of the British Empire in India, he became Governor of Bengal in 1765, introduced the first postage stamps, created a pension fund for disabled officers and reformed the civil administration.

especially chintz, Kashmir shawls with semi-abstract decorative motifs, Moghul car-pets and tent hangings.

There was also the customary presentation of gifts, and the Moghuls often chose expensive shawls and sashes from Kashmir, which became highly prized by the Company officials. Some of them ended up in various museums and exhibi-tions. Many are in private collections as heirlooms.

Trading mainly in gum, spices, indigo, raw silk, sugar, muslin cotton and saltpetre, the Company also employed local jewellers to make ornaments using Indian rubies, diamonds, garnet and chalcedony. Some of these precious stones were discovered in 1912, buried for 300 years under 30–32 Cheapside, London. The excavation came to be known as the Cheapside Hoard, with unanswered questions about its owner-ship as well as the mystery of its cover-up.

The Company secured the services of local artists and illustrators to record the flora and fauna of India, which they published in Britain to promote travel and trade to the subcontinent. They generated so much public interest that a new industry was born. Those travelling to India to see the exotic sites and visit the Hindu shrines were charged a 'pilgrim tax'. Mercifully, some of the revenue collected was used for the maintenance of the temples.

The 257 years of activities of the English East India Company in India, first as traders and then as rulers, came to an abrupt end with the Mutiny of 1857. The revolt necessitated the transfer of the Company's administration to the Crown. The casualties were not only the thousands of nameless sepoys and Mangal Pandey but also Jahnsi Ki Rani, a victim of Lord Dalhousie's Doctrine of Lapse, which gave the Company the right to take over any principality improperly administered, or when

The Taj Mahal, one of a set of 60 paintings of Indian monuments commissioned by the East India Company to promote tourism to the subcontinent.

the ruler died without a natural heir. Such was the case in the principality of Jhansi, where the Company broke its promise to accept Rani's adopted son as the heir to the throne.

With the disappearance of the Company's own army, the Government of India was transferred to the Crown and, by Royal Assent, the Board of Control was duly replaced by the Council of State for India. On 1st September 1858, the passing of the India Act gave an assurance to the princes of India that there would be no further encroachment on their lands and rights, and the East India Company's power came to an end.

But not without leaving its fingerprints on every aspect of life in India. It played a major role in introducing the English language in the country; its army became the army of British India, and the introduction of merit-based appointments became the model for the Indian civil service. However, the company remains accused of pillaging India in the name of trade: of transferring monies and treasures to Britain that not only made it rich but also helped the industrial revolution to take place in Britain. Without the East India Company, Britain would never have developed into the nation it is today.

The activities of the East India Company also changed the eating and drinking habits of the British. It was the lure of spices that led the English to go to India in 1600, and resulted in London becoming the biggest spice market of the world, with pepper – the 'black gold' – the most expensive seasoning. Other spices were used for medicinal as well as cooking ingredients. The great cookery writer Elizabeth David (1913–92), indeed, considered spices more important than food, often describing them as kings of the kitchen. In return, the British introduced to India vegetables from America such as potatoes, tomatoes and chillies. Curry powder became popular in Britain in 1780, and in 1810 the first Indian restaurant was opened in London by Sake Dean Mahomed, though it was not until the middle of the twentieth century that curry houses became a fixture in just about every town in Britain. Nowadays there are over 9,000 Indian restaurants in Britain, and curry has become one of the most popular foods, almost overtaking fish and chips.

The East India Company was also at the centre of the tea trade, and imported vast quantities of it into England. Because of the huge prices demanded, it was often smuggled into the country. Tea was such a great luxury that it was kept in ornate wooden boxes known as tea caddies which were locked and the keys kept away from the servants in case of pilfering. Tea is now the most popular beverage of the nation and enjoyed by all classes. A standby for all occasions, 'a nice cup of tea' can be reassuring, celebratory, or just plain refreshing.

With no more direct connection with India, the demise of the East India Company also meant the end of Haileybury School, the college founded in 1806 to train young men to work in India. The school was re-named Haileybury and Imperial Service College, and in 1896 a young Clement Attlee was a pupil, and said to have

Sake Dean Mahomed (1759–1851) opened The Hindoostanee Coffee House in 1810, the first Indian restaurant in London.

been 'intoxicated' by the large areas of the map of the world coloured red displayed there. This was at the height of the British Empire. Fifty-one years later, on 20 February 1947, now Labour Prime Minister, Attlee made a long and detailed announcement in Parliament that the British Government intended to withdraw all its military forces and government officials from India. In granting independence to India, Attlee caused his once-favourite colour to disappear from the map of India.

Policing

When the East India Company arrived in India in 1600, it retained the traditional Moghul policing system, which was mostly concerned with the protection of travellers and the safety of wealthy citizens against organised gangs of looters. The Company improved the organisation and the quality of the police agents, and Warren Hastings, who introduced British supervision over police work, created the first civil police force in India.

Sir Charles Napier, having conquered the Sindh, maintained law and order with a disciplined, armed and well trained police force. He formed the Sindh Police, modelled on the Irish Constabulary. It was a great success, with sufficient British Officers eventually becoming the famous Indian Police Commission in 1860. Under this Constabulary Policing System, the British officers were responsible for recruitment, training, discipline, internal economy and technical police work. They registered all criminal cases and investigations.

From 1861, India's police centre was governed by the Colonial Police Law. Since Independence, it has remained unchanged but not without criticism. It was originally legislated by the British in the aftermath of the Mutiny of 1857, with the intention of suppressing any movement for Indian independence. The law governs almost all police forces in India today.

Fingerprinting was introduced to India by Sir William Herschel (1833–1917) who arrived in 1853 to serve as Administrator of the East India Company and was then appointed Chief Magistrate in Bengal. In 1858, he began using fingerprints and handprints on documents such as deeds, business contracts, and jail warrants in the belief that they were more binding than signatures and the best method of preventing fraud in a society where illiteracy was high. He also discovered that they were unique and permanent and that no two fingerprints were the same. This created a method of individualisation capable of being used for accurate identification.

In 1897 the Council of Governor General approved a Committee report for the use of fingerprints for classification of criminal records. The Bureau of Calcutta became the world's first fingerprinting centre, run by Aziz Haque and Hem Chandra Bose. Herschel is credited with being the first person to see the value of the use of fingerprints and for its primary development in India and, subsequently world-wide.

Protecting the Seas

The Royal Indian Marine Service, established for the defence of Indian seas, dates back to the earliest days of the East India Company when two British ships, under Captain Best, arrived in Surat, India in 1612. Since then there has always been a sea service under the British Government in India.

In 1670, Bombay became the headquarters of the Service, with its own specially constructed ship-building yard. It was the skill of the family of Lovji Nasarwanji Wadia, who discovered the value of teak as a substitute for oak, that initially led to the huge success of Indian ship-building industry

Engaged in continuous warfare against the pirates, the Dutch, the Portuguese and the mutates, the Royal Indian Marine Service was constantly on active service. The ships 'flew the flag' with the white and blue ensigns and with the Star of India as a distinctive mark at the bow.

Following Indian independence in 1947, the Royal Indian Navy was divided between India and Pakistan and on 26 January 1950, when India became a Republic, the Royal Indian Navy was renamed the Indian Navy.

Creating a Voice

Newspaper publishing in India was first attempted by the East India Company in 1776 but without success. It was not until 1780 when James Augustus Hicky made publishing history by printing the *Bengal Gazette*, the first newspaper in India, an English-language weekly in Calcutta, the then capital of the British India. The 'father of the Indian journalism' intended to attract the attention of the local British population; his motto was: 'A weekly political and commercial paper open to all parties but influenced by none'.

Headquarters of the *Mumbai Samachar*, established in 1822.

Hicky made no secret of who he liked and who he criticised in the two page weekly. He wrote unfavourable vengeful articles about the East India Company. His outspoken critical comments about the wife of Governor-General Warren Hastings, and sharp confrontational remarks about the Governor himself and the Chief Justice too, did not go down well in the official households. In retaliation, Hastings denied Hicky the use of postal facilities 'for failure to promote England's economic interests', which was seen as a form of press censorship. Hicky's mounting debts resulted in him being imprisoned. Undaunted, he ran the paper from his prison cell, but not for long. The paper ceased publication in 1782. In 1799, Lord Wellesley brought the Censorship of Press Act with the sole purpose of stopping the French publishing any harmful criticism about the British.

The first Indian language newspaper was *Samachar Darpan*, in Bengali, published in 1818. The *Bombay Samachar* in Gujarati was launched in 1822 and is the oldest newspaper in Asia still in print.

Passports

The use of passports in India and the British Colonies was introduced after the First World War. The Indian Passport Act of 1920 established controls on foreign travels of Indians, restricted to the British Empire and some of the countries in Europe. The first passport consisted of a single folded page mounted within a cardboard cover. It was based on the format accepted by the 1920 League of Nations Conference of Passports.

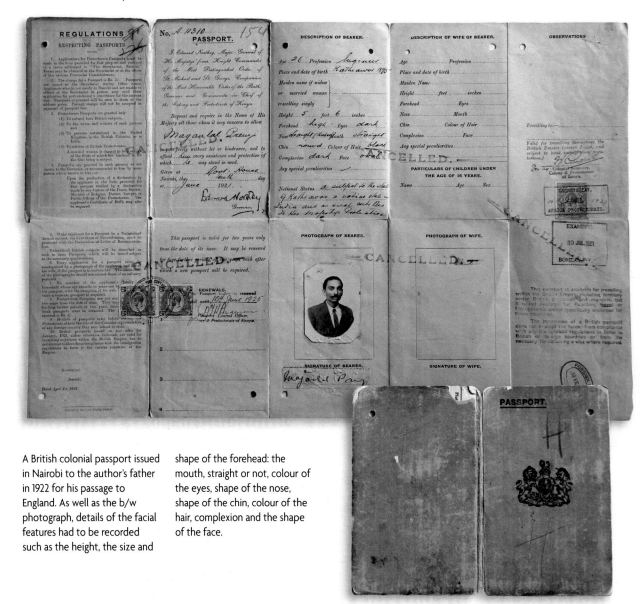

A British colonial passport issued in Nairobi to the author's father in 1922 for his passage to England. As well as the b/w photograph, details of the facial features had to be recorded such as the height, the size and shape of the forehead: the mouth, straight or not, colour of the eyes, shape of the nose, shape of the chin, colour of the hair, complexion and the shape of the face.

CHAPTER 3
Mutiny and Martyrs

The Black Hole of Calcutta

The Black Hole of Calcutta was a small dungeon in the old Fort William, Calcutta – the name 'Black Hole' originally being used by the British for any garrison lock-up used to confine drunken soldiers.

In 1756 a conflict broke out between the young and self-indulgent Nawab of Bengal, Siraj-ud-Daulah, and the British in the city, who had begun to fortify their settlement without his permission. The Nawab ordered its demolition; the British refused. They were also found to be abusing the trade privileges given to them. As a result, Siraj-ud-Daulah marched with a large contingent to the settlement, stole valuables from the British, and locked them up in the dungeon for the night to prevent them escaping. The cell was a mere 18 feet by 14 feet, with just one window. That night the temperature was unfortunately oppressive, and by morning 43 of the 64 captives had died of suffocation. Subsequent reports of 146 being locked up and

The 'Black Hole of Calcutta' was the name given to a small prison cell with one window. During a conflict in 1756 between the British and the Nawab of Bengal, the British began fortifying their settlement without the permission of the Nawab. He marched on them with a large contingent, stole British valuables and locked the captives in the dungeon to prevent escape. Following an oppressive night, 43 of the 64 prisoners were found dead.

23 surviving are no more than British mythology – there was no way so many could be accommodated in such a tiny space.

After the incident the Black Hole was demolished, and a memorial tablet was erected on the site, which later disappeared. In 1899 Lord Curzon, the Viceroy, commissioned a new monument; nationalist leaders, including Subhash Chandra Bose, subsequently campaigned for its removal, and in 1940 it was re-erected in the graveyard of St John's Church, Calcutta.

The Battle of Plassey, 1757

Although Robert Clive, the Commander in Chief of British India, had made peace with Siraj-ud-Daulah, he never forgot the tragedy of the Black Hole and was determined to take revenge. He also wanted to see Siraj-ud-Daulah deposed, so he could put Mir Jafar, the Nawab's commander-in-chief, in his place, and therefore hatched a conspiracy against the Nawab. Clive wrote a letter to Siraj-ud-Daulah setting out the grievances of the Englishmen in Bengal, and led his army towards Plassey. This was intended to provoke the Nawab to march his forces to Plassey to engage the British, but what the Nawab didn't know was that Mir Jafar would desert him, and join Clive with all the Nawab's forces under his command. Clive had created a dangerous situation but, having made his mind up to fight, he ignored advice not to proceed. His

Lord Clive meeting with Mir Jafar after the Battle of Plassey.

Tipu Sultan.

A bronze statue of the 'Tiger of Mysore' erected in memory of Tipu Sultan.

artillery created confusion for the enemy, which gave Mir Jafar the opportunity to come over to Clive. Twenty-two Englishmen and over 500 Indians lost their lives. Siraj-ud-Daulah ran away, but was captured and killed by the son of Mir Jafar.

Clive's victory at Plassey saw Mir Jafar assume the throne of Bengal and, through their enormous influence over him, the British establish a strong power base in that part of India. Their new military pushed out the other colonial powers, the Dutch and the French. Using Bengal as a base, the British now gradually took over the whole of India. They were no longer merchants: they became empire-builders, and it was Robert Clive who effectively founded that empire.

Tipu Sultan

Tipu Sultan (1750–99) is immortalised as the Tiger of Mysore, and forever associated with the mechanical tiger, specially made for him, which is now a prized exhibit at the Victoria and Albert Museum in London. The model tiger has an Englishman by the throat – not without reason, because Tipu hated the British, whom he fought 'tooth and nail'. The feeling was mutual: the British hated him as much as they dreaded him.

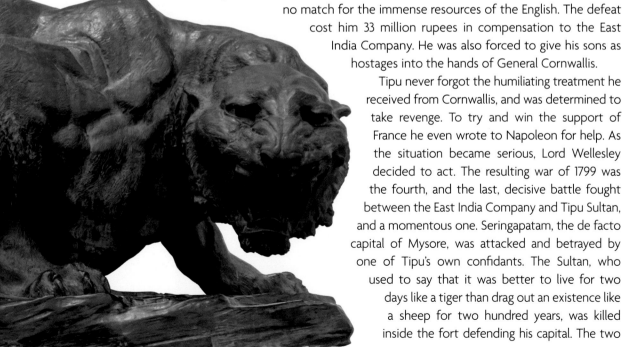

Over the years Tipu Sultan had purchased and built a large number of weapons and built up huge military might, all of which he brought to bear in 1792 in his war against the British. But for all Tipu's strength, his misfortune was that he was no match for the immense resources of the English. The defeat cost him 33 million rupees in compensation to the East India Company. He was also forced to give his sons as hostages into the hands of General Cornwallis.

Tipu never forgot the humiliating treatment he received from Cornwallis, and was determined to take revenge. To try and win the support of France he even wrote to Napoleon for help. As the situation became serious, Lord Wellesley decided to act. The resulting war of 1799 was the fourth, and the last, decisive battle fought between the East India Company and Tipu Sultan, and a momentous one. Seringapatam, the de facto capital of Mysore, was attacked and betrayed by one of Tipu's own confidants. The Sultan, who used to say that it was better to live for two days like a tiger than drag out an existence like a sheep for two hundred years, was killed inside the fort defending his capital. The two

One of the two brass 3-pounder guns captured by the British on 4 May 1799 at the Battle of Seringapatam in which Tipu Sultan was killed. Now on display at Sandhurst.

brass 3-pounder guns used in the battle were captured by the British forces during the storming of Seringapatam and brought to England, and now flank the entrance to the Officers' Mess at the Royal Military Academy at Sandhurst in Surrey, a permanent reminder of the conquest of India.

Mutiny

The darker side of the history of the British in India is represented by three mutinies: at Vellore, Barrackpore, and the Great Mutiny of 1857 at Lucknow.

The Barrackpore Mutiny near Calcutta in 1824 is seen as a rehearsal for the 1857 Mutiny. The rebellion was caused by the refusal of mostly high-caste Hindus to board boats to cross the polluting 'dark waters' to Burma. When their complaints were ignored, they rose up and drove away the British officers. Approached and asked to surrender, they refused. The British troops launched a full-scale attack on the Indian sepoys, killing 200, and executed their leader and hero, Binda.

But the seeds of the Great Mutiny of 1857 go back further still, to 1806, and the mutiny at Vellore, now in Tamil Nadu – the first instance of a large-scale and violent mutiny by Indian sepoys against the East India Company. It was resentment at a change in dress code ordered by the Commander-in-Chief that led to the outbreak. Instead of a turban, Indian troops now had to wear a round hat with leather and cocked feather, shave off their beards, trim their moustaches and wear leather stocks. They were also required to remove painted marks (*tilak*) from their foreheads, and wear no jewellery. This harsh order unsettled the Hindu and Muslim soldiers – for one

The Indian Mutiny, 1857.

Mangal Pandey.

thing, leather was the skin of cow or pig, and thus unacceptable to both Hindus and Muslims. The rebellion was provoked by the sons of Tipu Sultan of Mysore, who had been lodged at Vellore since their surrender at Seringapatam in 1799. The response was brutal: those who protested were given 90 lashes each and dismissed from the army. By way of revenge the sepoys killed more than 100 British soldiers. A massacre followed, and more than 350 rebels were killed by the British.

It is wrong nevertheless to describe the 1857 Indian Mutiny as the 'First War of Independence': it was a rebellion by Hindu and Muslim soldiers serving the East India Company. The military revolt was not an all-India uprising, but confined to the Bengal Army, and the most that could be said of it is that it lit a spark of nationalism throughout India as never before. The true significance of the Mutiny was that it inspired later freedom movements in the country. The scars of the rebellion run deep and remain distressful.

Its real cause was a rumour that the bullet cartridges provided to the troops – the ends of which had to be bitten off before they could be loaded into the soldiers' Enfield rifles – were greased with animal fat: cow and pig, forbidden by both the Hindu and Muslim religions.

A 29-year-old sepoy called Mangal Pandey (1827–57), led the call to rebel, vowing to shoot the first European in sight. As the mutiny spread, the British called the mutineers 'pandies'. Pandey eventually became involved in a firearms incident with a white officer, and tried unsuccessfully to kill himself. The British considered him a traitor; the Indians, a freedom fighter, which he certainly was not. In 1984, the Indian Government issued a postage stamp to commemorate him.

There followed more rebellions in other parts of India, Oudh and the North

West Provinces. After a temporary collapse of authority, the British responded with force and military superiority and defeated the rebels, whose last significant battle was fought at Gwalior, during which Rani Laxmibai of Jhansi was killed. The British then cracked down ruthlessly on dissent, lashing mutineers to cannons and blowing them to pieces.

The 1857 Mutiny was, however, a major turning-point in the history of India and Britain, leading to the dissolution of the East India Company in 1858, and the subsequent direct government of the country by the Crown as the British Raj.

The domed Indian Kiosk in the Queen's Garden at Frogmore, commemorates the end of the Mutiny in India in 1858.

Jhansi

Laxmibai, the Rani of Jhansi (1828–58), Queen of the princely state of Jhansi, was one of the most active and leading figures at the time of the 1857 Mutiny. For Indian nationalists she was the symbol of resistance to the rule of the East India Company. Educated at home, she received lessons in archery, horsemanship and self-defence. She married the Raja of Jhansi and, as they had no children of their own and the Raja was ailing, they decided to adopt a boy to succeed him. In spite of assurances given by East India Company officials, after the death of the Raja the adopted son was rejected by them as the legal heir. In such cases of States without successors, the Company usually invoked the Doctrine of Lapse and took them over – which is what it did with Jhansi. The annexation was an unbearable and quite unprecedented humiliation for the Rani. Through a British lawyer, John Lang, she appealed to the Directors of the Company, but lost. The British authorities now decided to punish the Rani for her presumptuous action, confiscating the state jewels, putting her on a pension and ordering her to leave Jhansi.

Statue of Laxmibai, the Rani of Jhansi and her adopted son, in Solapur near the Kambar Talav.

When the mutiny broke out in 1857, the Rani decided to show her courage and fearlessness by organising a revolt against the authorities. 'The battle plans were affected mainly under the direction and personal supervision of the Rani of Jhansi,' wrote the Times of India's correspondent, 'who, clad in military attire and attended by a picked and well-armed escort, was constantly in the saddle, ubiquitous and untiring.'

On 5 June 1857 mutinies broke out at both Jhansi and nearby Gwalior. The Rani, dressed in her regular cavalry uniform, led her army and for some time defended Jhansi against the Central Indian Field Force under the command of Hugh Rose, the first Baron Strathnairn (1801–85). She fought hard, holding her reins in her mouth so that she would wield her swords in both hands.

According to one version of her death, the Rani was hit by a series of bullets as the British launched their assault. As she lay mortally wounded, dressed in red jacket, trousers and white turban, she gave her ornaments to be distributed among her loyal troops.

Rani, the 'Joan of Arc' of India, quickly became a cult figure, and a symbol of armed resistance to the British rule in India. A statue of Field Marshall Hugh Rose on horseback was erected in his memory in Knightsbridge in London, and moved in 1931 to Griggs Green in Hampshire.

Rose massacred the entire population of Jhansi, and went on to defeat the mutineers at Lahore and Gwalior. For his eminent service he was promoted to the rank of Lieutenant-General, then Commander-in-Chief of the Bombay Army, and in 1860 he was made the Commander-in-Chief in India.

Jallianwalla Bagh, 1919

The massacre of hundreds of men, women and children at Jallianwalla Bagh, Amritsar, on 13 April 1919 at the hands of Brigadier-General Reginald Dyer (1864–1927), was a turning point in the history of Anglo-Indian relations. The worst atrocity committed during the regime of Sir Michael O'Dwyer (1864–1940), the Governor of Punjab, it has stained the image of British rule in India forever. Worse still, it was only five months after the end of the First World War, in which thousands of Indian soldiers, many from Punjab, had died in defence of Britain.

At the time there was a nationwide *hartal* (lock-out or strike) in India, without much success, and a proclamation was issued against the holding of public gatherings. Many people, mostly villagers, and probably unaware of the proclamation, assembled at Jallianwalla Bagh to celebrate Baisakhi, the spring Punjabi festival. The authorities took no steps to prevent the gathering. Without giving any notice to disperse, General Dyer then gave orders to the troops to fire into the crowd, which they continued doing until they ran out of ammunition. Three hundred and seventy-nine people were killed, and 1,200 wounded. Governor-General O'Dwyer cut off water and electricity supplies to Amritsar and ordered many people to be flogged. A humiliating 'crawling order' was issued on the street where an English woman was assaulted by an angry mob, seeking revenge on the capture of two Indians on 10 April. Anyone entering the street between 6am and 8pm was made to crawl for 200 yards on all fours. The order was effective between 19 and 25 of April.

In London the Hunter Committee of Inquiry was set up to investigate the facts surrounding the massacre and apportion blame. It rejected Dyer's justification of the indiscriminate killing – that he feared other rebellions could be triggered throughout India on the scale of 1857 – condemned his behaviour, and asked him to resign his command and return to England. Not everyone in Britain, however, was

against Dyer's actions. A debate in the House of Lords went in his favour by 35 votes. Encouraged by Sir Michael O'Dwyer, the *Morning Post* launched a fund for 'The Man who Saved India' and raised over £26,000 'to comfort him in his dying days'. The most unexpected and unbelievable donation, of £10, came from Rudyard Kipling (1865–1936), who thought that the Empire was a moral cause.

Among the outraged Indians was the newly knighted Rabindranath Tagore, who returned the honour to the Viceroy, particularly to signify the contempt in which he held the crawling order. '*I wish to stand shorn of all special distinctions by the side of those of my countrymen who,*' he explained, '*for their so-called insignificance, are liable to suffer a degradation not fit for human beings*'.

Another Indian, the political revolutionary, Udham Singh (1899–1940), who had been present at Jallianwalla Bagh serving water to the families gathered there, witnessed the massacre and never forgot the sheer helplessness of the victims. He made up his mind to take revenge by killing Sir Michael O'Dwyer who, as Governor of Punjab, had supported the indiscriminate killing of innocent men, women and children.

For the next two decades Singh planned and prepared for the assassination of the Governor. He travelled to London and attended the meeting on 1 April 1940, when O'Dwyer was scheduled to speak at Caxton Hall, to what is now the Royal Society of Asian Affairs. He opened fire on O'Dwyer just as the meeting came to an end and shot him twice. Singh made no attempt to flee; he was charged with the murder, convicted, and hanged at Pentonville Prison. In 1974 his remains were exhumed, and taken to India to be cremated.

At his trial at the Old Bailey, when asked for his motive to murder the Governor, Singh replied: *I did it because I had a grudge against him. He deserved it. For 21 years, I have been trying to wreak vengeance. I am happy that I have done the job. I am not scared of death. I am dying for my country. What greater honour could be bestowed on me than death for the sake of my motherland?*

Above far left: The memorial marking the position of the Company troops when they opened fire on the innocent crowd.

Above centre: The memorial to those killed at the Jallianwalla Bagh, 1919, has the following inscription: '*This place is saturated with the blood of about a thousand Hindu, Sikh and Muslim patriots who were martyred in a non-violent struggle to free India from the British domination.*'

Above: Udham Singh, Indian revolutionary assassinated Governor Michael O'Dwyer to take revenge on the massacre at Jallianwalla Bagh. He was hanged at Pentonville Prison, London in 1940.

Bhagat Singh (1907–31) was a revolutionary involved in the struggle against the rule of the British Raj. As a teenager he visited the site of the Jallianwalla Bagh only hours after the massacre, which deeply disturbed him, and he collected soil from the spot which he kept with him all his life.

Rejecting the non-violent movement of other nationalist leaders, Singh joined those who advocated direct action as a means of overthrowing the British government in India. His aim was to establish a Republic of India by means of revolution, becoming a most popular and prominent of Indian freedom fighters.

When Lala Lajpat Rai was violently attacked while leading a peaceful anti-Simon Commission demonstration in Lahore in 1928, and died two days later, Singh exacted revenge by shooting the British police officer responsible. Evading capture he then helped to plan a bomb attack on the Central Legislative Assembly in Delhi. The intention was not to cause death or injury but to draw attention to the suppression and suffering of the Indian people. Instead of running away, he surrendered and was imprisoned, where he went on a hunger strike demanding equal rights for both the British and Indian political prisoners.

The result was nationwide support and Singh became a symbol of the new awakening among the youth. In a letter to the Viceroy, Lord Irwin, Singh asked to be treated as a prisoner of war and to be executed by firing squad and not by hanging. Four days before, a letter of clemency was presented to Singh which he declined to sign. His last words were, 'Down with British Imperialism'. His legacy prompted the youth in India to continue fighting for independence.

Bhagat Singh is commemorated with a large bronze statue in the Indian parliament and every year on 23 March, Martyr's Day, he is remembered as one of the heroes of the struggle.

General Reginald Dyer who was severely criticised by the Hunter Committee of Inquiry.

Sir Michael O'Dwyer, Governor of Punjab, who was assassinated in London at the Caxton Hall, immediately after his address to the Royal Society of Asian Affairs.

Bhagat Singh refused the offer of clemency and is regarded as a martyr to the cause of Indian independence.

CHAPTER 4
Moghuls and Monarchs

In 1526, the Moghul Chief of Kabul, Zahir al-Din Muhammad Babur (1483–1530), invaded India and fought against the ruler of Delhi, Sultan Ibrahim Lodi, in the Battle of Panipat. Lodi was defeated and the victory of Babur marked the beginning of the Moghul Empire in India, during the reign of Henry VIII (1491–1547).

During the 331 years of their rule, 19 Moghul Emperors played prominent role in the affairs of the country as powerful military leaders, patrons of arts and science and as administrators. For some, their power was not without family rivalries, resulting in murders and abdications.

Queen Elizabeth I (1558–1603) granted the Royal Charter to the English East India Company in 1600, and sent a letter to Emperor Akbar requesting permission to trade in his dominions in terms as good as those enjoyed by the rivals, the Portuguese, who had been in India since 1503.

Akbar The Great (1556–1605), grandson of Babur ruled as Moghul Emperor in the reign of Queen Elizabeth I. He was a brilliant General and an outstanding administrator who greatly expanded the Moghul Empire, ultimately taking control of the whole of India. An enthusiastic patron of science, poetry, painting, literature and architecture, he was regarded as the most illustrious ruler of the Empire and remembered along with Emperor Ashoka (304–232BC) the greatest ruler India has ever seen.

Moghul Emperor Jahangir (1605–27) succeeded his father Akbar the Great at the age of 36, and was amongst the most interesting of the great Moghuls. Sir Thomas Roe, England's first envoy to India, was sent by King James I to arrange a commercial treaty with the Emperor for the East India Company. It was to give them exclusive rights to reside and build factories in Surat. Roe presented his credentials to the Emperor in 1616 and remarked: 'He is a very affable and of cheerful countenance … and not proud in nature … the wisdom and goodness of the king appears above the malice of others…'. In return the Company offered to provide the Emperor with rarities from European markets. Jahangir sent a long reply to the King, ending with,

Jahangir, Moghul Emperor from 1605–27, during the reign of King James I. He is depicted with a halo indicating a divine nature.

'For confirmation of our love and friendship, I desire your Majesty to command your merchants to bring in their ships of all sorts of rarities and rich goods fit for my palace; and that you be pleased to send me your letters by every opportunity, that I may rejoice in your health and prosperous affairs; that our friendship may be interchanged and eternal'.

King James I (1603–25) came to the English throne, when the East India Company was already established in India. He was keen to increase England's revenues from India, and in 1614 appointed Sir Thomas Roe (c.1581–1644) as England's first envoy to the Moghul Court with the aim of securing trading agreements with India. This was also the year when the arrival of an Indian in England, was officially recorded for the first time. The reign of King James I will forever be associated with the beginning of the Indo-British relationship at an official level.

Shah Jahan (1628–58) came to the throne when the Moghul power was at the height of its prosperity, with control of the vastly wealthy provinces of Gujarat and Bengal. His was also the golden age of architecture and the beautiful ceremonial of the imperial assembly, the Durbar. The most famous example of Moghul architecture, the Taj Mahal, was the tomb for Shah Jahan's favourite wife, Mumtaz Mahal and took 17 years to complete. In 1644 his beloved daughter was badly burned, and was treated by one of the surgeons of the English ships. Overcome with gratitude, the Emperor granted the surgeon his wish to establish a factory at Hooghly, Calcutta, as a reward.

Not impressed by his charm or warmth of friendliness, Sir Thomas Roe avowed of the young Shah Jahan, 'I never saw so settled a countenance nor any man keep so constant a gravity, never smiling, or in fact showing any respect of or deference of men, but mingled with extreme pride and contempt for all...'

Aurangzeb (1658–1707), son of Shah Jahan, who ruled most of India for nearly half a century, was the wealthiest of the Moghuls. In 1686 the East India Company was unsuccessful in getting permission from the Emperor to trade throughout the Moghul Empire. The British demand resulted in the so-called Child's War, which they lost. The Company sent envoys to Aurangzeb to plead for pardon. They had to prostrate themselves before the Emperor, pay a large indemnity, and promise better behaviour in the future.

In 1695 Aurangzeb was again provoked into attacking the English following a pirate raid of a Grand Moghul convoy near Surat. This time, a livid Aurangzeb agreed to a compromise. He asked the Company to make financial reparations, estimated at £600,000. He also shut down four of the Company's factories, imprisoned the workers and their captains, and threatened to end all English trading in India until the pirate was found. The raider successfully eluded capture in spite of a large reward offered by the Privy Council and the Company.

The Taj Mahal, Agra, India.

By the end of the 17th century, the East India Company had boldly established itself around the coast of India. In 1702 Aurangzeb's men failed to maintain his authority over the English settlement in Madras, and his death, at the age of 90, saw the split of the whole Moghul Empire into small kingdoms.

King George II (1727–60) and **Emperor Alamgir II** (c.1699–1759). It was during their reigns that India lost its status as an independent nation following the Battle of Plassey in 1757. Gradually, the Moghul Emperor's influence diminished until they were reduced to mere servants of the British. To keep up appearances they were allowed to participate in ceremonies and processions, but held no power.

King George III (1760–1820) appointed Warren Hastings as Governor-General of India in 1772. The Regulating Act for India was passed in 1773, the first step along the road to government control of India. In 1783, Edmund Burke MP introduced the India Bill, proposing that the government would govern and the East India Company would deal with trade. This dual system of control worked for the next 74 years until the Mutiny of 1857 when Parliament took over the responsibility of India.

Bahadur Shah II (1837–62) was the last Moghul Emperor during the dominant period of the East India Company. For his public support for the Mutiny of 1857 he was tried for treason and found guilty. He was saved the death sentence and instead

The Double Mohurs gold coin, issued in 1834. (National Numismatic Collection, National Museum of American History).

exiled to Burma in 1858, where he died aged 87. The East India Company, too, not only lost the power to rule India, but also brought an end to one of the greatest dynasties of the world.

King George IV (1820–30), whose statue is in Trafalgar Square – with another one outside the Royal Pavilion, Brighton – was instrumental in the foundation of the National Gallery and King's College, London. He appointed Sake Dean Mahomed as his personal shampooing surgeon. In India, Lord William Bentinck, who was Governor-General, believed that Indians should have more say in the running of their affairs.

King William IV (1830–37) came to the throne a year before the arrival of Raja Ram Mohan Roy, the first Indian on an official visit to England on behalf of the Moghul Emperor Akbar II. One of the reforms of King William's seven-year reign was the abolition of slavery across almost the entire British Empire. In 1835, the Royal Mint commissioned King William IV Double Mohurs gold coins to be produced in India going into circulation the following year. Lord Thomas Macaulay went to India in 1834 to serve on the Supreme Council of India. As a leading member of the Law Commission, Macaulay's creation of a Penal Code remains the founding document of Indian law.

The Royal Pavilion, Brighton was commissioned by the Prince Regent and completed in 1823 after his coronation as King George IV in 1820.

Queen Victoria (1837–1901) reigned for twenty years before the horror of the 1857 Mutiny, which led to the end of the 258-year rule of the East India Company when all control and government passed to the British Crown. In 1877 Victoria was proclaimed Empress of India, and assured her new subjects that 'the Indian people should know that there is no hatred to a brown skin'. Following her death, Lord Curzon initiated a massive public fundraising appeal to build the Queen Victoria Memorial in Calcutta, as a fitting tribute to her reign. It remains one of the largest monuments of the Raj.

King Edward VII (1901–10), Emperor of India, might have lived and worked in India had Gladstone, the Prime Minister, been successful in urging Queen Victoria to find the then Prince of Wales an official appointment there. In 1875–6 the Prince went on a tour of India, where he was entertained by the Indian government in Bombay and Calcutta and played sports with the Indian princes, which strengthened the ties between them and British royalty. The Prince helped to organise the Colonial and Indian Exhibition of 1886 and was instrumental in founding the Imperial Institute to celebrate Queen Victoria's Golden Jubilee in 1887.

King George V (1910–36), Emperor of India, made an extensive tour of the country as Prince of Wales in 1905–6. After his Coronation in 1911 he made a State visit to India with Queen Mary (1867–1953), for the magnificent Durbar in Delhi, where he announced that India's capital would be moved from Calcutta to Delhi. During the First World War the King paid a public tribute to the courage of the Indian soldiers fighting in Europe.

King George VI (1936–52) was the last Emperor of India, and the first head of the Commonwealth. He inherited the British throne unexpectedly, and it was during his reign that the break-up of the British Empire took place, starting with India in 1947. He remained as King of India and Pakistan, but the title 'Emperor of India' was abolished in June 1948. On his death in 1952, Princess Elizabeth became Queen Elizabeth II.

Queen Elizabeth II, (1952–) has never been the Head of State of India, but remains head of the 53-member Commonwealth of Nations of which India is the largest founding nation. She has consistently taken a keen interest in the nation's affairs, visiting India in 1961 for the first time, then in 1983 for the Commonwealth Conference, and again in 1997.

Queen Victoria and her Munshi

In the long history of Indo-British relationships, none has ever matched in warmth, intimacy and longevity, the friendship between Queen Victoria (1819–1901) and Abdul Karim (1863–1919). The story of their extraordinary relationship, and of the influence a commoner and servant came to have on the monarch, is not new. It has been reported and described over and over, both during Victoria's lifetime and in the many years since, in biographies, newspapers, journals, cartoons, books and documentaries.

Queen Victoria, never visited the 'jewel in the crown' of her empire, but nevertheless, after her accession as Empress of India in 1877, and subsequently, the additional title, Kaiser-I-Hind, she developed a passion for all things Indian. Her first-hand information about, and experience of the people of her beloved colony came exclusively through visiting Indian dignitaries and other Indians she met in Britain. Whilst she never went to India, the Queen arranged that India came to her, favouring many Indian servants, on whom she depended for information about their homeland.

The most prominent among these was Abdul Karim who came from Agra with Mohammed Baksh around the time of the Queen's Golden Jubilee in 1887. Following her first meeting with them, the Queen wrote in her diary, 'Baksh ... very dark with smiling expression' and 'Abdul ... very much lighter, tall with a fine serious countenance. They both touched my feet'.

In spite of his humble origins, the Queen took to Abdul immediately, appointing him Groom of the Chamber. He rapidly gained the favour and confidence of the Queen, who, in 1888 promoted him to be her private secretary, a Munshi, with access to official correspondence and state documents. She discussed Imperial affairs with him, and asked his advice on matters of policy. The general opinion among historians and researchers is that Abdul did not deal with any confidential state documents, nor was he privy to any sensitive political papers.

The Queen also presented Abdul with numerous gifts and allowed him the use of a carriage for his personal use, which immediately raised his status to the level of members of the royal household. Later, the Queen also built a cottage near the Castle on the Balmoral Estate for him and his wife, named after him.

Queen Victoria's admirer often accompanied her on visits to Scotland and Europe. Abdul gave the Queen regular lessons, teaching her to write Urdu and to speak Hindustani, to enable her to make polite conversation with princely visitors from India. Soon she started a diary in Hindustani and developed an interest in Indian literature.

Abdul also introduced the Queen to Indian curry, which she enjoyed greatly. Through this increasingly close friendship, Abdul brought a taste of the Indian way of life, food and language to the Queen's daily life. Although they met everyday, the Queen also wrote letters to Abdul regularly, closing with 'Your loving mother' or 'Your affectionate mother'. Some letters were also signed in Urdu.

Abdul's closeness to the Queen and the influence he had on her, caused concern and resentment at court as well as in the royal household: the issue of inequalities of race and class as well as his proximity to the Queen, were considered to be unacceptable and inappropriate. The honours she bestowed upon him were deemed to be quite out of order for a mere secretary. Abdul would have preferred a knighthood but had to settle instead, for lesser titles. In the Honours list of 1895, he was appointed a Companion of the Order of the Indian Empire (CIE). On Victoria's 90th birthday in 1899, he was further appointed Commander of the Victorian Order (CVO).

Abdul remained by the Queen's side until her death in 1901. He was the last person to view Victoria before her coffin was closed: he was then allowed to join others in the funeral procession.

Soon afterwards however, he was asked to return to India. *The Black and White* Magazine on 27th April 1901 reported:

Queen Victoria and Munshi Abdul Karim.

'Munshi Abdul Karim is returning to India after many years of faithful service as Queen Victoria's Indian Secretary. King Edward has presented the Munshi with a silver pen and ink case'.

What the journal did not report was that Abdul was summarily dismissed, severing all his associations with the court and royal household, including confiscation and destruction of all his letters from the Queen and unceremoniously despatched to India. He died in his hometown aged 46.

Portraits and a bust of Abdul, specially commissioned by the Queen, adorn her favourite place, the Durbar Hall in Osborne House on the Isle of Wight where they have fascinated thousands of visitors for over a century.

CHAPTER 5

Governor-Generals, Viceroys and Secretaries of State

In 1773, the Regulating Act created the office of Governor-General of Bengal, and in 1833, under the Saint Helena Act, a Governor-General of India was appointed. After the Mutiny, when the rule of the East India Company came to an end, the Government of India Act of 1858 created the office of Viceroy of India in addition to that of Governor-General. A new India Office was also created in London headed by the Secretary of State for India, a member of the Cabinet. The title of Viceroy was abolished in 1947 when India and Pakistan became independent, but the title of Governor-General continued to be used for the two dominions until 1950 and 1956 respectively.

The Governors, 1773–1950

Warren Hastings, Governor of Bengal from 1772 and Governor-General from 1773 to 1785, profoundly shaped later attitudes towards the government of British India. He had great respect for the ancient Indian scriptures of Hinduism and governed by referring back to the earliest precedents. He supported the founding of the Bengal Asiatic Society, which became a storehouse for knowledge about the subcontinent. On leaving India Hastings declared that 'I have saved India from foreign conquest. I have become the instrument of raising the British name'. When he returned to England, however, instead of the hero's welcome he had hoped for, he found himself facing an impeachment trial for crimes of misdemeanour committed during his time in India.

Warren Hastings.

Sir John Macpherson (1785–86) held the post temporarily for a very short time.

The Marquess Cornwallis (1786–93) followed the policy of non-intervention in the affairs of the Indian States enshrined in Pitt's India Act. He defeated the great Tipu Sultan, ruler of Mysore. He subsequently held the post again for three months in 1805.

Sir John Shore (1793–98) also followed a policy of non-intervention.

Sir Alured Clarke (1798–98) held the post temporarily.

Earl of Mornington (1798–05) was called 'the father of the Civil Service in India', opening a college to train the East India Company's servants in Calcutta.

The Marquess Cornwallis (1805)

Sir George Hilaro Barlow Bt. (1805–07) gave back Gwalior and Gohud to Scindhia.

Lord Minto (1807–13), Viceroy and Governor-General, entered into the Treaty of Amritsar with Maharaja Ranjit Singh.

The Marquess of Hastings (1813–23) completed the work started by Warren Hastings and initially continued the policy of non-intervention, but later found that danger from many quarters made it impossible.

John Adam (1823) became the acting Governor-General for seven months, and introduced censorship of the press.

Lord William Bentinck responsible for many of the landmark social reforms in India.

Lord Amhurst (1823–28) held office during the first Anglo-Burmese war and the capture of Bharatpur after the death of the Raja.

William Butterworth Bayley (1828) held the post for four months as acting Governor-General.

Lord William Bentinck (1828–35) increased appointments of Indian judges, introduced educational reforms and social changes, and abolished *suttee* and female infanticide.

Sir Charles Metcalfe Bt. (1835–36) abolished the restrictions on the Indian press.

Lord Auckland (1836–42) set up medical colleges at Bombay and Madras, and passed an act establishing equal rights for Indians and Britons in civil law suits.

Lord Ellenborough (1842–44) brought the first Afghan war to an end, and annexed Sindh to the British Empire.

Charles John Canning, 1st Earl Canning, was Governor-General of India during the Mutiny of 1857. When power was transferred to British Government, he became the first Viceroy.

William Wilberforce Bird (1844) was acting Governor-General for one month only.

Sir Henry Hardinge (1844–48) led a military campaign against Maharaja Duleep Singh which culminated in the Treaty of Lahore in 1846.

The Marquess of Dalhousie (1848–56) annexed the Punjab, creating a British province and took control of Nagpur, Jhansi and Oudh, he also introduced railways and the electric telegraph to India.

Viscount Canning (1856–58) reorganised India's legal, financial and administrative systems, withdrawing the Doctrine of Lapse, and established universities in Calcutta, Bombay and Madras. The Mutiny of 1857 took place in the second year of his Governorship. He became the last Governor and first Viceroy of India in 1858.

Earl Mountbatten was the last British Governor-General of India, 15 August 1947 – 21 June 1948. He did a lot of work in connection with the Indian States, persuading them to join the Dominions of India and Pakistan. His success averted the complications the rulers of the two newly independent countries would have faced.

Chakravarti Rajagopalachari (1948–50) was the first and only Indian national to hold the office of Governor-General of India, overseeing the transfer of India from dominion status to republic on 26 January 1950. He wanted to continue as the first president of the new republic, but withdrew following opposition from some sections of the Indian National Congress for his non-support of the 'Quit India' movement.

Chakravarti Rajagopalachari the only Indian to hold the office of Governor-General 1948–50, during India's transition to a Republic.

47

The Viceroys, 1858–1947

Viscount Canning (1858–62), initially appointed Governor-General, he became the first Viceroy of British India. Withdrew the Doctrine of Lapse.

Lord Elgin (1862–63) studied a multitude of problems involving regional and religious groups, holding a series of Durbars to meet rulers of different parts of the country.

Sir John Lawrence (1864–69) presided over India's telegraphic connection with Europe, and saw high courts established in Calcutta, Bombay and Madras.

Lord Mayo (1869–72) established the college at Rajkot in Gujarat and Mayo College in Ajmer for the Indian princes. In 1871 a census was held in India for the first time in history; a statistical survey of India was also organised. A year later he became the only Viceroy to be murdered, by a Pathan convict in the Andaman.

Lord Northbrook's term of office (1872–76) coincided with the Kuka movement in Punjab led by Sri Satguru Ram Singhji, an anti-British organisation that pioneered the tactic of non-co-operation.

Lord Lytton (1876–80) was known as the Viceroy of Reverse Characters. In 1877 he organised the Grand Delhi Durbar to decorate Queen Victoria with the Kaiser-i-Hind, and a year later he passed the infamous Vernacular Press Act, aimed at better controlling Indian-language newspapers.

Lord Ripon (1880–84) was sympathetic to Indians, improving primary and secondary education, aiming to prohibit child labour, and in 1883 passing the

Far left: Lord Mayo, the only Viceroy to be assassinated, while on a visit to the Andaman Islands.

Left: George Frederick Samuel Robinson, 1st Marquess of Ripon, educationalist and reformer.

George Nathaniel Curzon, 1st Marquess Curzon of Kedleston.

He was responsible for the Ancient Monument Protection Act (1904) and the restoration the Taj Mahal, and later for the unpopular partitioning of Bengal in 1905.

Lord Minto (1905–10) was Viceroy at a time of great political unrest in India. He passed various acts to curb the activities of extremists like Lala Lajpat Rai, Ajit Singh and Tilak, who were all imprisoned in the Mandalay jail in Burma.

Lord Hardinge (1910–16) held a Durbar in 1911 to celebrate the coronation of George V. He cancelled the partition of Bengal and moved the capital from Calcutta to Delhi. During his Viceroyship Annie Besant announced her Home Rule Movement.

Lord Chelmsford (1916–21) issued the August Declaration in 1917 for control of India's government to be gradually transferred to the Indian people. His tenure included the Government Act and Rowlett Act of 1919, and coincided with the Jallianwalla Bagh Massacre and the non-cooperation movement, and the foundation of the Women's University at Poona.

Lord Reading (1921–26) suppressed the non-co-operation movement. His period of Office included hosting a Royal visit by the Prince of Wales in 1921; and the formation of the Swaraj Party.

Lord Irwin (1926–31) was Viceroy during the period that saw the Simon Commission visit India in 1928, Gandhi's Salt March at Dandi in 1930, the civil

Ilbert Bill to enable Indian judges and magistrates to try European criminals, though it was later repealed.

Lord Dufferin (1884–88) saw the formation of the Indian National Congress in 1885.

Lord Lansdown (1888–94) brought in the Factory Act of 1891 and organised holidays for the workers.

Lord Elgin (1894–99) His spell of office included the great famine of 1896.

Lord Curzon (1899–05) was, at 39, the youngest ever Viceroy. He passed the Indian Coinage and Paper Currency Act (1899); put India on the gold standard and extended the railway system. He organised famine relief; passed the University Act in 1904 and increased official contributions to the universities.

disobedience movement, and the First Round Table Conference in England in 1930.

Lord Willingdon (1931–36) held office during the Second Round Table Conference in London in 1931, and the Third in 1932. The Government of India Act was passed in 1935.

The Marquess of Linlithgow (1936–43) implemented plans for local government. The Second World War broke out while he was Viceroy; Congress ministers resigned; there was massive civil disobedience in India; the 'Quit India' Movement saw its leaders imprisoned; Linlithgow was blamed for the famine in Bengal.

Lord Wavell (1943–47) arranged the Simla Conference with the Indian National Congress and the Muslim League, which failed to reach an agreement. Elections for a Constituent Assembly were held and an interim government was appointed under Nehru.

Lord Mountbatten was the last Viceroy of British India, serving from February to August 1947 and the first Governor-General of an independent India. He found himself having to oversee the partition of India, Pakistan and India becoming two separate independent nations. This followed the passing of the Indian Act of 1947 which legalised what had been promised to the people of India. After that, the British Government was to have no control over the internal affairs of the two countries.

Above: Victor Alexander John Hope, 2nd Marquess of Linlithgow.

Left: Field Marshal Archibald Percival Wavell, 1st Earl Wavell.

Below: Lord Louis Mountbatten, 1st Earl Mountbatten of Burma.

Secretaries of State for India (1858–1947)

The post of the Secretary of State for India was created in 1858 when the rule of the East India Company came to an end after the Mutiny of 1857 and the era of the Colonial period began under the British rule- the Raj. The Secretary became the Political head of the India Office in London and had responsibility for the governance of India for the next 89 years. As a result, The Board of Control and the Court of Directors were abolished and their powers given to the Secretary of State for India and his India Council. India was the only country in the Empire to have such a patronage to itself.

Lord Stanley 15th Earl of Derby.

There have been 33 Secretaries of State for India between 1858 and 1947 with terms of office ranging from a few months to eight years. The first Secretary of State for India was **Lord Stanley** (1858–59). He had charge of the India Bill of 1858 in the House of Commons and had an excellent reputation as a man of ability and fairness.

Those who followed him were,

Sir Charles Wood (1859–66)

The Earl de Grey (1866)

Viscount Cranbourne (1866–67)

Sir Stafford Northcote (1867–68)

Duke of Argyll (1868–74)

The Marquess of Salisbury (1874–78)

The Viscount Cranbrook (1878–80)

The Marquess of Hartington (1880–82)

The Earl of Kimberly (1882–85)

Lord Randolph Churchill (1885–86)

The Earl of Kimberley (1886)

Viscount Cross (1886–92)

The Earl of Kimberley (1892–94)

Henry Fowler (1894–95)

Lord George Hamilton (1895–1903)

William St John Brodrick (1903–05)

The Viscount Morley (1905–10) Writer and newspaper editor, whose dealings with the Raj combined statesmanship and patience.

The Earl of Crewe (1910–11)

The Viscount Morley (1911)

The Earl of Crewe (1911–15)

Austen Chamberlain (1915–17)

Edwin Samuel Montague (1917–22) led the delegation to Paris Peace Conference in 1919. He was responsible for the Montague-Chelmsford Reforms which led to the Government of India Act 1919, committing the British to the eventual dominion status of India.

The Viscount Peel (1922–24)

The Lord Olivier (1924)

The Earl of Birkenhead (1924–28)

The Viscount Peel (1928–29)

William Wedgwood Benn (1929–31)

Samuel Hoare (1931–35) negotiated the Government of India Act 1935 and was regarded as the most effective parliamentarian in putting the India Independence Bill through the House of Commons.

The Marquess of Zetland (1935–40) was very much involved with the affairs of India and played an important role in Government of India Act 1935.

Lord Amery (1940–45) had a long disagreement about the future of India and saw the British Empire as a force of justice and progress in the world. He wanted the United Kingdom, India and Pakistan to be united in trade.

Lord Pethick-Lawrence (1945–47) was involved in the negotiations that led to India's Independence in August 1947

The Earl of Listowel (1947–48) was the last Secretary of State for India seeing the emergence of India and Pakistan as two independent nations. His last formal duty was to inform King George VI at Balmoral, that the transfer of power to Indian hands had been successfully completed. The title of George VI, Rex Imperator could be used no more. All that remained was for him to return to the King the ancient seals,the badge of the Secretary of State's Office, the emblem linking the Indian Empire to the British Crown. Unfortunately, having been misplaced some years before, there were no souvenirs to return. The King lost the jewel in the crown as well as the proof of its ownership at the stroke of midnight on 15 August 1947.

The original Foreign Office building in King Charles Street, London, that included the India Office, the Colonial Office and the Home Office. It was completed in 1868 and opened by Prime Minister Benjamin Disraeli, MP. It is now the Foreign and Commonwealth Office. On the steps is the Grade II listed bronze statue of Robert Clive, originally unveiled opposite Gwydyr House in Whitehall in 1912 and moved to its current location in 1916.

Clive of India

Robert Clive (1725–74) earned the title Clive of India for his victory at Plassey in 1757, which laid the foundations of British power in Bengal and provided the basis for further expansion into the interior of the country. Lord Clive's career in India can be briefly summed up as; merchant, soldier and statesman. Although he did not completely purify the administration, he initiated and maintained reforms of considerable magnitude. Others saw Clive as 'a man of insight rather than of foresight'.

Robert Clive went to India in 1743 after being offered a clerical job with the East India Company. Later, when the British and French were fighting for supremacy, the Company summoned him and he secured the British forces in Madras. He then moved on to Calcutta and recaptured it from the Nawab of Bengal, Siraj-ud-Daulah, and early in 1757 gained control of Bengal. A few months later, having defeated the Nawab at the Battle of Plassey, he was declared the conqueror of India. In 1765 Clive became Governor of Bengal, where he reformed the civil administration, restored military discipline, pensioned off the Nawab of Bengal, and created a pension fund for disabled officers. In 1766 he introduced the first postal system in India, initially for official purposes only, but this was extended to the general public in 1837.

Robert Clive, 1st Baron Clive, by Nathaniel Dance.

Clive returned to England in 1766 to meet resentment from the politicians for his accumulated wealth from India, which led to a parliamentary inquiry. He became an opium addict and is said by some, to have committed suicide, although other opinion has it that he died a natural death.

'To Clive', said Viceroy Lord Curzon, 'we owe the fact that there has been an India for Englishmen to serve and for British Viceroys to govern. Forgive him his errors, they were great but never mean; remember his achievements that were transcendent; shed a tear over the final scene – it was tragic but not ignoble. After all, was not Clive the first of the Indian Pro-consuls to suffer from the ingratitude of his countrymen and did he not thereby inculcate a lesson and set an example that has taught others to endure?' Lord Macaulay's verdict was more succinct: 'Our island has seldom produced a man more truly great than Robert Clive, either in arms or in Council.'

A statue of Robert Clive stands outside the former India Office building in Whitehall, now the Foreign & Commonwealth Office. As well as the huge amount of money Clive brought from India, he collected many treasures, including a tent which had belonged to Tipu Sultan. Many of these items are now on display at the Clive Museum at Powys Castle in Wales, the largest private collection of this type in Britain..

CHAPTER 6
Indologists and Orientalists

Not all who went to India were traders, nor were they all merciless in extracting monies from the local communities. During the rise and fall of the Moghul rulers there was almost an exodus of great British intellectuals to India. The passion for India and its culture felt by British Indologists and Orientalists in turn led to India's classical civilisation being revealed to the West. Even Warren Hastings, the first Governor-General of India, was a scholar who respected Indian values and stated that, 'The people of this country do not require our aid to furnish them with a rule of conduct or a standard for their property.' In 1780, with James Hicky, he started the *Bengal Gazette,* the first major newspaper in India; to 'inform and amuse' the public.

In 1784 the Asiatic Society of Bengal was founded, and soon came to be appreciated deeply by Indians grateful for its pioneering work in re-discovering their country's great intellectual heritage. Its founder, Sir William Jones (1746–94), was an Orientalist and jurist who went to Harrow and Oxford, where he was an outstanding scholar, and learned Latin, Greek, Hebrew and Persian. He was knighted and went to India as Judge of the Supreme Court in Calcutta in 1783. Within four months of his arrival in the country and with the idea of founding an institution for the study of Oriental literature and culture, the Asiatic Society, a museum had been established in Calcutta.

Bust of the Sanskrit scholar Henry Thomas Colebrooke created by Henry Weekes in 1837.

Jones learned Sanskrit in order to understand Hindu law and translated *Shankuntala, Hitopadesha,* the *Gita* and *Manusmriti,* and extracts from the *Vedas* into English. His knowledge of Sanskrit symbolised the best of English relationship with India. He also published works on Indian law, music, literature and geography. Jones's invaluable contribution to Indian philosophy, religion and literature is considered by some to be 'the most outstanding achievement of the Indian civilisation'. During his lifetime, Jones learned no less than 28 languages, including Chinese.

Other eminent Orientalists included Charles Wilkins (*c.*1750–1836), who published a translation of the *Gita* and of the *Hitopadesha*; H H Wilson (1766–1860), who translated the *Vishnu Purana* and *Rigveda*; and H T Colebrooke (1756–1837), who published in a similar field. German scholars contributed, too, in propagating India's great works to an international audience – Indologists like Max Müller (1823–1900), Albreacht Weber (1825–1901), who published *Vajasanevi Samhita,* and Rudolf Roth (1821–95), who published *Atharvaveds* as well as *The Literature and the*

Right: Thomas Macaulay,
1st Baron Macaulay.

Far Right: Friedrich Max
Müller.

Brahmi script.

History of the Vedas. It was not until 1834 that James Prinsep (1790–1840), the founding editor of the *Journal of the Asiatic Society*, deciphered the Brahmi script used in the Ashoken decree which provided the key to early Indian history.

Amongst the great Sanskrit scholars were Sir Monier Monier-Williams (1819–99), E B Cowell (1826–1903), George Buhler (1837–93). V A Smith (1848–1920) and M Elphinstone (1779–1859) who pioneered the writing of Indian history. The greatest Oriental scholar is acknowledged to be Henry Thomas Colebrooke, who published *A Digest of Hindu Law* and also famous essays on the *Vedas*.

In 1793 the English Baptist missionary William Carey went to India, and subsequently translated the Bible into Bengali, Sanskrit and several other Indian languages. He was successful in converting 700 Indians to Christianity and laid an impressive foundation of education and social reforms.

All these distinguished British and German scholars established the greatness and magnificence of India's glorious past.

Unlike his predecessors, the Orientalists who favoured the Indian classics, Thomas Babington Macaulay (1800–59), 1st Baron Macaulay, believed passionately that the language of education in British India should be English, and made the greatest contribution to its establishment as such, indeed to introducing the western concept of education there.

Lord Macaulay went to India in 1834 after a successful career in British politics, to take up a well-paid post in the Supreme Council of India, and recommended the

William Carey.

replacement of Sanskrit and Persian with English as a more suitable language for the teaching of history, science and technology. His *minute* became the basis of reform introduced in the English Education Act of 1835. 'It is the genius of this man,' wrote the scholar and journalist K M Pannikar, 'narrow in his Europeanism, self-satisfied in his sense of English greatness, that gives life to modern India as we know it. He was India's new Manu [Manu Samhita, whose writings during the first two centuries AD were the text that inspired ancient Hindu law], the spirit of modern law incarnate.'

Cornelia Sorabji (1866–1954) also defended Lord Macaulay's proposals to make English the common language in India. During her address at the Royal Institute of International Affairs on 24 October 1940 she said,

'Lord Macaulay who has met with a great deal of abuse at the hands of those who have not taken the trouble to read his despatches concerning the common language being English. If you read those despatches, you will find that the Indians themselves asked that the language should be English, partly because the Indians of those days were Anglophiles and partly because they realised that it would be difficult to find an Indian language which would be acceptable to everyone ... and if England was genuine in wanting us to take part in our own government later on, English was the best language we could have...'

CHAPTER 7
Travellers and Botanical Science

The botany of India became an enduring interest of the British. In 1787 Colonel Robert Kyd (1746–93), the Military Secretary to the Bengal Government, founded of the Botanical Gardens in Calcutta, which by 1790 had over 4,000 plants being cultivated and in blossom. The other forum for botany in Calcutta was the Asiatic Society founded by Sir William Jones in 1784. His objective was to enquire 'into the history and antiquities, arts, science and literature of Asia', which included becoming an important forum for the exchange of botanical information and drawings. With his knowledge of and interest in Sanskrit, Sir William Jones was keen to 'give Indian plants their true Indian appellations'. One of the Society's members, William Roxburgh (1751–1815), a botanist and surgeon, was appointed Superintendent of Calcutta Botanical Gardens, eventually publishing many works relating to Indian botany. He is said to have been the first botanist to commission local artists to draw watercolours of locally grown plants, employing two of these painters at his own

Two examples of the botanical illustrations commissioned by the East India Company, *Bombax ceiba* (right) and *Costus speciosus* (far right).

expense. They produced nearly 700 drawings, 300 of which were put into his book *Plants of the Coast of Coromandel*, with detailed descriptions of the plants from Madras. Each life-size drawing had to be not only attractive, but also scientifically accurate and educational. His style was adopted by succeeding illustrators under the patronage of the East India Company.

By the time William Roxburgh left India, he had collected 2,542 botanical drawings, which are now in the Botanical Garden in Calcutta, and known as the Roxburgh Icons. The work undertaken by him was described as 'the most beautiful and correct delineations of the flowers ever seen. Indeed the Hindoos excel in all minute work of this kind.'

Marianne North (1830–90), nicknamed the Flower Huntress, was a painter with an unparalleled energy and interest in travel and identifying and recording tropical crops and flowers from all over the world. She embarked on her overseas journeys in 1871 and in 1877 went to India for two years. She painted temples, palm trees and exotic flowers, first in south India and later in the north and north-east. These are included in over 800 of her drawings exhibited in the Marianne North Gallery at the Royal Botanic Gardens in Kew, London, built at her own expense. Travelling by pony, log cart, carriage, steamer and railway, Marianne North also wrote about her excursions in India, giving most vivid and colourful accounts of her encounters with the locals. Her travels were not always without danger to herself and her companions.

While artists recorded their impressions of India on canvas, others put pen to

Above: Marianne North

Far left: *Bauhinia variegata*.

Left: The Indian Coral Tree, *Erythina variegata* which is said to have been stolen from the Celestial Gardens by Lord Krishna and has since been under a curse, which is why it is never used in Hindu worship.

Thomas Coryate travelled mostly on foot but wrote, '*I have rid upon an elephant since I came to this Court, determining one day (by Gods leave) to have my picture expressed in my next Booke, sitting upon an elephant'.*

paper and published books of great historic value about what they saw and experienced. The first English person to do so was the writer, traveller and adventurer Thomas Coryate (*c.*1577–1617), who walked 5,000 miles to India in 1615. Employed by King James I's oldest son, Prince Henry, as a 'court jester' before he went to India, Coryate was the first westerner to visit the country with no thought of either trade or conquest. He went around India on foot, wearing oriental clothes, and was called an 'English Fakir'. He wrote with wit and spirited inquiry about local cultural activities and their strange marriage customs. Some of his letters and books were published in 1616.

Coryate had brought with him a letter of introduction to the Moghul Emperor Jahangir and presented it to him at Court. He praised the Emperor and impressed him with his oratory in Persian. By way of appreciation, the Emperor rewarded Coryate with one hundred rupees. It was also at the Court that Coryate met Sir Thomas Roe, the first English envoy to India.

The first English travel writer, and a great pedestrian of his time, Coryate never complained of the hardships of his walkabouts. However, the climate and his exertions finally proved too much. Following fainting spells, he managed to make his way to the East India Company's hospitality in Surat where, suffering a bad stomach brought on by an English diet of too much local beer and meat in hot weather, he died. His death making him the first English tourist to die in India.

The most archetypal modern-day writer, traveller and adventurer in India was, of course, Mark Shand (1951–2014), brother of Camilla, Duchess of Cornwall. His passion for the endangered Indian elephant took him to India to protect it, and he travelled all over the world to raise money for its welfare. He wrote the bestseller *Travels on my Elephant*, with Tara the elephant as its leading lady. Shand featured in many documentaries about elephants to raise awareness of the need for the conservation of their species. An Indophile, he was deeply interested in Indian culture and religion and, like Thomas Coryate before him, he too travelled all over India, not on foot but on the back of an elephant. The adventures of these two remarkable men are separated by four hundred years but united in their determination to explore the world with admirable courage.

CHAPTER 8
British Friends of India

Edmund Burke a vociferous critic of the East India Company and its methods of governing India.

'This is the story of the British friends of India, not the story of the Empire. It celebrates the contributions of those who battled for the larger cause of freedom and gives credit where it is due. It pays homage to remembrance of British scholars, administrators, statesmen and many others who made common cause with those who struggled for fairness, justice and freedom. This is a panoramic view of the Indo-British relationship in perspective. The vignettes and episodes in this book represent an aspect of Britain which we all in India applaud and appreciate. To give accolade to those who saw India as a civilisation and who saw the freedom struggle of India as a legitimate imperative during the colonial period imparts a golden touch to the celebration of 50 years of our Independence and is an abiding contribution to Indo-British friendship.' Dr L M Singhvi, Indian High Commissioner to the United Kingdom 1997, in the foreword to *India – British-Indian campaigns in Britain for Indian reforms, justice and freedom 1831–1947*, published in the Golden Jubilee year of India's Independence

Edmund Burke (1729–97) was a British statesman, politician, philosopher and a great parliamentarian. Though he never went to India, he maintained a keen interest in the country. Being in opposition to the government of the day he had no say in how India was ruled, but was most critical of those who did. He strongly believed that it was wrong and inappropriate for India to be ruled by England. The East India Company, Burke felt, was governing India in a deplorable manner and invading its culture, for which its employees should be punished.

He singled out Warren Hastings as the target for his campaign, and in 1788 impeached him, the trial taking place in Westminster Hall in front of Queen Charlotte, the Prince of Wales, members of both Houses of Parliament and the President of the Royal Academy, Sir Joshua Reynolds.

Burke's prosecuting speech took four days to present to the court. He accused Warren Hastings of undermining the rights of Indians and criticised the way taxes were collected, often by extortion; women were often abused and mutilated, others stripped of their clothes, exposed to the public and whipped. Burke's verdict was that Hastings was the 'captain-general of iniquity' who never dined without 'creating a famine', whose heart was 'gangrened to the core', and who resembled both a 'spider of Hell' and a 'ravenous vulture devouring the carcases of the dead'.

The case attracted large numbers of the public, prepared to pay as much as 50

William Carey.

A view of the tryal of Warren Hastings Esqr. before the Court of Peers in Westminster Hall on an impeachment delivered at the Bar of the House of Lords by the Commons of Great Britain in Parliament assembled February 13, 1788. Drawn by E. Dayes, engraved by R. Pollard, aqt. by F. Jukes. (Library of Congress).

Below: The plaque in Westminster Hall.

ON THIS SPOT
WARREN HASTINGS
STOOD HIS TRIAL 1788-1795
HE WAS ACQUITTED
ON ALL THE CHARGES

guineas per ticket. The trial dragged on for seven years, on and off, the East India Company meeting the cost; the letters and journals of Jane Austen show that she knew Hastings and followed the trial. But public interest waned, and eventually the House of Lords acquitted Hastings, to Burke's great disappointment. However, the trial did succeed in establishing the principle that the Empire ought to be a moral undertaking, rather than a wholesale looting by the East India Company or its members.

William Carey (1761–1834), known as the 'father of modern missions', went to India in 1793 at a time when the East India Company was in control of India and hostile to the missionaries. Landing at Calcutta. Carey went to work in a factory, where he had a chance to preach and teach. He translated the entire New Testament into Bengali dialect to reach the masses. During his 41-year stay in India, Carey became Professor of Sanskrit at Fort William College and also preached in Bengali. He became the Editor of *Ramayan* and compiled dictionaries of various Indian languages and translated Indian scriptures.

In 1799 Carey witnessed the *suttee*, the burning of the widow at the funeral of her husband, and, deeply moved, he implored the English government to put an end to the ritual. It wasn't until 1829, however, that Lord William Bentinck, the

T 3582.   A HINDU MARRIAGE.

Governor-General, with the support of Raja Ram Mohan Roy, signed the necessary edict and sent it to Carey to translate into Bengali for publication. On receiving the request, Carey exclaimed, 'No church for me today; if I delay an hour to translate and publish this, many a widow's life may be sacrificed'. The authorities had the translation the same day.

Postcard showing a child groom on his wedding day aged 3.

Lord Bentinck (1774–1839) had been appointed Governor-General of Bengal in 1828, with the priority of reducing the English East India Company's losses. *Suttee*, which had been practised since 1,700 BC, the Vedic Ages, was just one of the cruel Indian social customs, of which he was critical, along with polygamy, the rigid caste system and child marriages. With his Chief Captain, Sir William Sleeman, Bentinck also put an end to *thuggi*, the organised crime of the early 19th century in India, which robbed, maimed and killed millions of wayfarers, and made travel in India highly dangerous. The history of *thuggi* goes back to 1326. An extensive campaign was started in 1835 and over 1,400 thugs were caught. Some were hanged, others transported for life. In 1839, Meadows Taylor published a popular novel, *Confessions of a Thug*. Even Queen Victoria became interested, to the extent that she asked for each chapter to be sent to her as it was being corrected by the author.

Lord William Bentinck.

As Governor-General, Bentinck made sweeping social, economic and political reforms that laid the foundations for modern India. He reformed court procedure and made English, rather than Persian, the language of the higher courts, with the aim of encouraging the spread of western-style education to prepare Indians to serve in the British bureaucracy.

Florence Nightingale (1820–1910), the founder of modern nursing, came to prominence while serving in the Crimean War, where she was named 'the Lady with the Lamp' by wounded soldiers. Although she never went to India she had a long-lasting interest in Indian medical and social conditions, corresponding regularly with officials there and collaborating with the Viceroy Lord Ripon (1880–84) for nearly 40 years on issues of hygiene, clean water and sanitation. Her book of letters to Prasanna Kumar Sen (1937) between 1878 and 1882 shows how concerned she was about living conditions in deprived areas. At a public meeting in Norwich in 1873, Florence Nightingale read out a paper on the health situation in India. Following the establishment of the Indian National Congress in 1885, she wrote a letter to Allan Octavian Hume on the eve of its first meeting in Bombay (now Mumbai) welcoming the 'birth of a new nationality'. In a letter to Sir William Wedderburn on 27 November 1885, she wrote:

Florence Nightingale, never travelled to the subcontinent, but corresponded regularly with the Viceroy Lord Ripon about the problems of hygiene and sanitation in India.

> *Mr Hume who brought me a letter from Mr Ilbert was so good as to give me a good deal of his time. This 'National Liberal' Union, if it keeps straight seems altogether the matter of great interest that has happened in India, if it makes good progress, perhaps for a century. We are watching the birth of a new nationality in the oldest civilisation in the world. How critical will be its first meeting at Poona; I bid it God speed with all my heart I could wish (but you know my opinion is worth nothing in this kind of political policy).*
>
> *bless you and your work.*
> *Ever yours faithfully,*
> *F. Nightingale*

Florence Nightingale also discussed the Indian political situation in India with delegates from the Indian National Congress, and in 1889 contributed to a special fund for Cornelia Sorabji's studies at Somerville College, Oxford. Cornelia subsequently went to visit Florence Nightingale in London. On her death in 1910 Florence Nightingale gave Sir William Wedderburn a legacy of £250 for 'some Indian object'.

George Yule (1829–92) was a Scottish merchant living in England who went out to India in 1875 to join his brother. There he served as Sheriff of Calcutta and as President of the Indian Chamber of Commerce. Like other British friends of India, Yule joined in the protest against British imperialism and the unacceptable ways in which it manifested itself on Indian territory. He became a member of the Indian National Congress,

George Yule was a tireless campaigner and first European President of the Indian National Congress.

and within three years was elected president, the first non-Indian to hold that office. In Britain he was on the British Committee of the Indian National Congress and the Editorial Board of its journal, *India*.

Allan Octavian Hume (1829–1912) A retired civil servant who regarded himself as a 'Native of India', founded the Indian National Congress in 1885. He saw the INC as a political club of volunteers, but it quickly developed into a democratic mass movement that dominated the political scene in India. The conflict was always with the Empire as a system, not with the British people. The Congress had many British sympathisers and supporters fighting for India's cause, including George Yule, Sir William Wedderburn, Henry Cotton, Alfred Webb, Annie Besant and Nellie Sen Gupta, all of whom became its Presidents. They also helped set up a 'British Committee of the Indian National Congress' in London for the express purpose of informing the public about conditions in India and the ways of the British bureaucracy there.

Allan Octavian Hume founder of the Indian National Congress.

Alfred Webb (1834–1908), an Irish Nationalist and Member of Parliament, frequently visited India as a messenger of peace and goodwill, and became a close friend of Dadabhai Naoroji, who in 1894 invited him to preside over the Indian National Congress. Webb supported *Anti-Caste*, the first British journal about anti-racism, founded in 1888, which exposed and condemned racial prejudice across the British Empire and the United States, and drummed up subscribers and activists for it around the world. Together with Naoroji, Webb co-signed a letter backing a new association called the Society for the Furtherance of Human Brotherhood.

Charles Bradlaugh (1833–91) was one of the 'Voices in Parliament' who consistently put the case for the Indian National Congress and India's freedom. He was a keen supporter of Annie Besant, who distributed countless pamphlets to those interested in the relations between India and Britain.

Alfred Webb.

Sir William Wedderburn Bt (1838–1918) was a Bombay High Court judge, Member of Parliament at Westminster (1884–87) and a distinguished member of the Indian Civil Service, who played a leading part in the establishment of the Indian National Congress and was its president in 1899 and 1910. His work for Indian independence was as important in India as it was in England. 'Vast masses of India are altogether unrepresented,' he declared at a luncheon gathering at the National Liberal Club in London: 'They have no voice in the management of their own affairs. Now they have found a voice in the Indian National Congress through which to address the people of England.' In 1890 he launched *India: The Voice of the Indian National Congress* in England, for the discussion of Indian affairs, and paid for its running costs whenever there was a shortage of funds. Throughout his life he never missed any India-related meetings anywhere in the country.

Right: Charles Bradlaugh.

Far right: Sir William Wedderburn.

Henry Cotton (1845–1915), a civil servant went to India in 1867 and took up a series of official appointments in Bengal including Revenue Secretary and member of the Bengal Legislative Council. He supported Home Rule for India and served as President of the Indian National Congress in 1904. Cotton opposed Curzon's partition of Bengal and often spoke about Indian matters in Parliament. He became the Chief Commissioner of Assam and in 1901 established the Cotton College there. In 1911 he wrote his memoirs, *Indian and Home Memories*. 'Young India can never forget the service of Sir Henry Cotton,' said Lala Lajpat Rai (1865–1928), from his exile in Tokyo in 1915, 'and when the history of New India will be written, I am sure Sir Henry's name will find an honoured mention.'

Annie Besant (1847–1933), a prominent Theosophist and women's rights activist went to India in 1893 and stayed there, getting involved with the nationalist movement. Her whole life was dedicated to the cause of India and was often imprisoned for her political activities. In 1916 she started the Home Rule for India movement, which later became the India League, making quite clear her belief that home rule was the birthright of the people of India. The following year she became the President of the Indian National Congress. In her speech she said, *'For the first time in Congress history, you have chosen as your President one, who, when your choice was made, was under the heavy ban of Government displeasure, and who lay interned as a*

person dangerous to public safety....' Politics apart, Besant took a keen interest in education and founded the Central Hindu College at Banaras in 1899 and translated the *Bhagavad Gita* from Sanskrit into English. She died in India.

Charles Freer Andrews (1871–1940), better known as C F Andrews, was an educator who took an active part in the Indian independence movement. His sense of justice was aroused by the humiliating conditions of Indians in South Africa. Teaching philosophy at college in India, he grew close to the students, and was dismayed by the racist behaviour and treatment of the Indians by the British officials. Elected president of the All-India Trade Union, becoming involved with the activities of the Indian National Congress, he was affectionately known as 'Deenabandhu', a friend of the poor. He helped the 'Swaraj' movement and in 1912 met Rabindranath Tagore in England. He also completed the job of abolishing indentured labour in Fiji, that had been started by Gopal Krishna Gokhale before his untimely death.

Bertrand Russell (1872–1970) British philosopher, logician and Nobel laureate was a champion of anti-imperialism and a friend of Nehru.

Agatha Harrison (1885–1954) was University Welfare Tutor at London School of Economics and visited India in 1929 with Royal Commission on India. She was Secretary of the India Conciliation Group in 1950 and was greatly interested in the activities of the India League.

Above left: Henry Cotton was a firm supporter of Indian self-rule and became President of the Indian National Congress in 1904.

Centre: Annie Besant, women's rights activist and founder of 'Home Rule for India'.

Above: Charles Freer Andrews.

Right: Mrs Nellie Sen Gupta, an English woman who married an Indian and became a fervent campaigner for independence and President of the Indian National Congress.

Centre: Baron Reginald William Sorenson.

Far right: Michael Foot, Cabinet Minister and Leader of the Labour Party who was a lifelong supporter of the Indian cause in Britain.

Mrs Nellie Sen Gupta (1886–1973) married an Indian and went to live in India, joining him in India's struggle for freedom. She addressed mass meetings and was often imprisoned for breaking the law, and in 1934 was elected President of the Indian National Congress. After independence she went to live in East Pakistan (now Bangladesh), in her husband's home town.

Baron Brockway (1888–1988) born in India was Chairman of Movement for Colonial Freedom and a vocal supporter of India's struggle for freedom.

Reginald William Sorenson, Baron Sorenson (1891–1971) Labour Party politician was a critic of the harsh means by which the British rulers were striving to maintain their Empire in India. At the Labour Party Conference in 1933 he spoke out saying, *'The operation of imperialism in India is in essence no different from the operation of Hitlerism. We are appalled at what is happening to the Jews in Germany, but what has been happening in India is just as bad.'*

Harold Laskey (1893–1950) a British political theorist, economist, author and lecturer at the London School of Economics with notable Indians, V K Krishna Menon and K R Narayan as his students. He was a keen supporter of the independence of India. The Indian government established The Harold Laskey Institute of Political Science in 1954 at Ahmedabad in, Gujarat, in his honour.

Michael Foot MP (1913–2010) was a Labour Member of Parliament and eventually leader of the party, in which capacities he was a brilliant orator, as well as a distinguished journalist and author, and a lifelong proponent of India's cause in Britain. He was Chairman of the India League, founded by Krishna Menon (1896–1974), and President of the Indian National Congress Centenary Celebrations Committee in UK in 1985, chairing its Gala Dinner in London.

CHAPTER 9
Constructions Good and Bad

In their efforts to exploit the vast wealth of materials and resources available in India, the British set about a massive programme of infrastructure projects. In order to transport men and materials and to communicate efficiently over great distances, they covered the country with a network of railways, roads, canals and telegraph systems. Large areas of dry land were made fertile by some of the world's greatest irrigation schemes. The railways cut travel times and the new improved roads, helped transport goods in larger quantities. The introduction of the telegraph meant greatly improved communication and the publication of the first regular weekly newspaper, the *Bengal Gazette* which could mobilise public opinion. These developments were all considered necessary to attract further British investment in India.

An army of Victorian civil engineers with responsibility for completing these bridges, tunnels, canals, dams, roads and railways, was brought to India by Lord Dalhousie, the Governor-General. He established a Department for Public Works which oversaw all construction projects. He made every effort to add to the British dominion of India earning him the title of, 'Builder of the British Empire'.

The Ganges Canal, Roorkee, Saharanpur District. The brainchild of Sir Proby Cautley; construction began in 1840, and the canal was opened by Governor-General Lord Dalhousie in April 1854.

Irrigation in India: Britain's Contribution

Compiled and edited by Jeremy Berkoff,
from *Epic Engineering*, by Alan Robertson

Irrigation in India dates back thousands of years – there are few types of irrigation that do not have their origins in ancient practice. For millennia, farmers have installed hand-dug wells, village tanks, small-scale diversions and mountain terraces; major delta works originated under the Chola kings, one of the longest ruling dynasties in the history of South India around the first century AD, and included the remarkable Grand Anicut on the Cauvery, the oldest dam in the world, built during the 2nd century AD over the river Cauvery (also spelt Kaveri). There are large inundation canals and possibly controlled diversion projects that date back at least to the Indus Valley civilization, with both types extensive in Moghul times. As far back as 1568, Akbar's Canal Act sets out responsibilities and rules for major diversion works which in 1845 Baird Smith said had 'solved many of the problems... now pressing on ourselves.'

So what did the British bring? In three words: scale, organisation and technology. Their initial interventions concentrated on restoring and extending pre-existing works. These were soon followed by far larger schemes requiring the mobilisation of thousands of workers and the development of new techniques of surveying, design and construction. Two pioneering examples were the Ganges Canal and the Godavari Barrage, both meriting inclusion, indeed, in Alan Robertson's book *Epic Engineering*. And epic they were. Commencing at the holy city of Haridwar,, the Ganges Canal was some 700 miles long, and supplied surface irrigation to almost two million acres in the Ganges-Jumna *doab*. With a capacity of 6,750 cubic feet per second, the canal was of an order of magnitude greater than any other canal built anywhere in the world to date. The Godavari Anicut, modelled on the Grand Anicut to the south, more than two miles long, irrigated 650,000 acres in the famine-affected delta of the largest of the south Indian rivers.

Though both projects were on a scale that dwarfed anything that had gone before, the great engineers who conceived them, Proby Cautley for the Ganges Canal and Arthur Cotton for the Godavari Barrage, had so little prior experience to go on that, like their Moghul and Chola forebears, they were obliged to adopt a trial-and-error approach. Mistakes were made, most notoriously, Cautley's misplacement of a decimal point in the design of his canal which led to its capacity inadvertently being

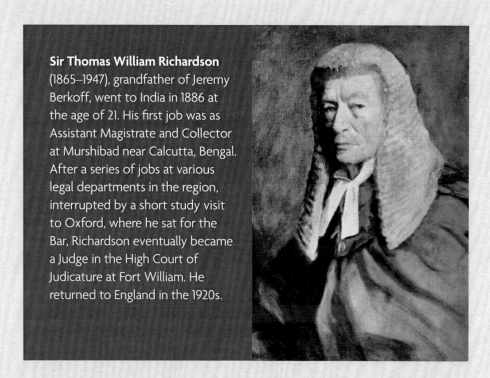

Sir Thomas William Richardson (1865–1947), grandfather of Jeremy Berkoff, went to India in 1886 at the age of 21. His first job was as Assistant Magistrate and Collector at Murshibad near Calcutta, Bengal. After a series of jobs at various legal departments in the region, interrupted by a short study visit to Oxford, where he sat for the Bar, Richardson eventually became a Judge in the High Court of Judicature at Fort William. He returned to England in the 1920s.

tripled! Over time, however, such problems were resolved, if not by them then by their successors, and to this day both projects continue to operate much as designed.

Moreover, the ground was laid for a massive expansion of the irrigation system, first by the British and then by subsequent governments. Huge new areas were developed, notably in the Punjab and Sindh – to the extent that some 90% of all arable land in Pakistan is now irrigated – and in the deltas of Eastern India and Burma. The total area of the sub-continent equipped for irrigation has risen to more than 220 million acres, about three times the combined area in 1947, and accounting for perhaps 45% of the cultivated area. Moreover, irrigated land in general is much more productive than rain-fed land, so agriculture remains highly dependent on irrigation.

That said, irrigation in the sub-continent is a continuing story. Despite major technical and related advances, large-scale projects face numerous administrative, operational and environmental problems that neither the British nor successive governments have been able adequately to resolve, and it is the farmers themselves who have come closest to finding the solution. Throughout the period of British rule, small-scale farmer irrigation remained the most widespread sector, and its contribution has been greatly strengthened since independence by the introduction of mechanical drilling and pumps. Today, groundwater accounts for more than 50% of the irrigated area: given the control this provides to the farmers, it now plays a critical role in feeding the huge populations of the region.

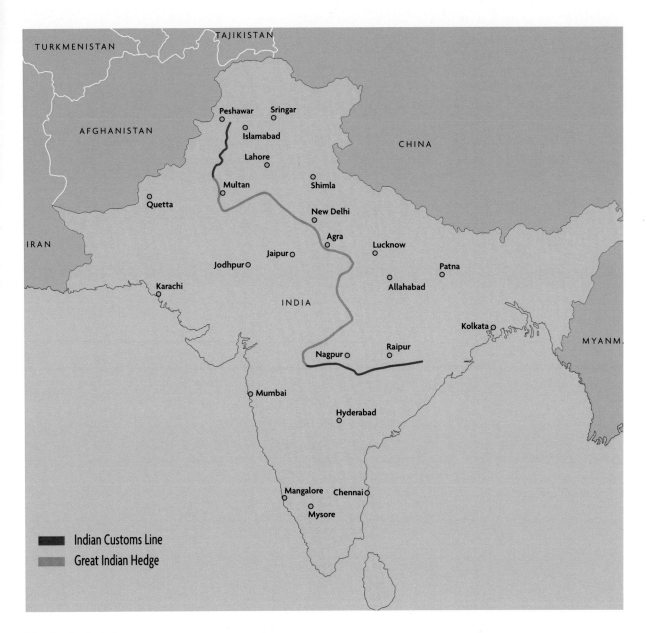

Map showing the Indian
Customs Line and the Great
Indian Hedge.

The Great Indian Hedge

Until recently the history books have made little reference to the Great Indian
Hedge. And yet it was one of the most extensive man-made structures in India, and
comparable only to the Great Wall of China.

In fact, it was a customs line, created in 1840 by the East India Company with the
aim of preventing the smuggling of salt to avoid the much-hated salt tax. Stretching

71

for 2,500 miles from the edge of Himalayas all the way to Orissa, the hedge was 14 feet high, and 6 to 12 feet wide. It was made of closely clipped trees and, in places, stone walls, and guarded along its length by 12,000 men.

A common home-grown condiment salt, had no justification for being taxed, but its taxation in India, which the East India Company increased to swell their profits, dates back to the earliest times, and the practice continued even after the administration of India was transferred to the Crown in 1858. Public outrage found a voice in 1885 when the matter was raised in the First Session of the Indian National Congress and described as 'a monstrous system to which it would be almost impossible to find a parallel in any tolerable civilised country.' In 1930 Gandhi organised a protest march from Ahmadabad to the beach at Dandi, deploring the salt tax as 'inhuman', but, like other subsequent protests, it was not successful, and it was not until 1946 that the much-hated tax was abolished by the Interim Government of India.

'In populated parts of the country, where smuggling is rife, the men are active in preventing the passage of contraband goods by a barrier which, in its most perfect form, is utterly impassable to man or beast and all the outlets through which, are guarded.'

Allan Octavian Hume, Commissioner of Inland Customs

'To secure the levy of a duty on salt ... there grew up gradually a monstrous system, to which it would be almost impossible to find a parallel in any tolerable civilised country. A custom line was established which stretched across the whole of India, which in 1869 extended from the Indus to the Mahanadi in Madras, a distance of 2,300 miles; and it was guarded by nearly 12,000 men ... it would have stretched from London to Constantinople ... it consisted principally of an immense impenetrable hedge of thorny trees and bushes.'

Sir John Strachey, distinguished member of the Indian Civil Service, 1842

Railways

One of the first engineering projects planned and executed by the British in India, and in covering the entire country also the largest, was the railway network. Before that, with poor and dangerous road conditions, the only means of transport was the bullock cart or the horse carriage. Palanquins were for royalty and the rich. Two and a half centuries after the East India Company set foot in India, it saw the need for an improved means of transport to move troops around the country and deliver cotton to the ports for shipment to England, as part of a wider strategy of improving trade between India and Britain.

Initially, the Company built a short experimental line in 1835 at Chintaripet, near Madras, to carry construction material for the dam on the river Godavari. At such an early stage, the problems of working in heavy rain and gusty winds, the intensity of the heat, the effect of tracklaying on the vegetation and, most importantly, the need to find skilled and reliable engineers, were all major considerations. But all this was overcome, and the line was opened in 1837.

The success of the experiment gave the company the confidence to build the first passenger line between Bombay and Thana, 21 miles apart, inaugurated on 16 April 1853 amidst loud cheering and a 21-gun salute. The 14-carriage train had three loco-motives, appropriately named *Sultan*, *Singh* and *Sahib*, and carried 400 VIPs on a historic journey of one hour and fifteen-minutes. On 15 August 1854 the first passenger service ran between Howarth and Hooghly in Bengal, the large crowd present fascinated to see the 'fire-breathing horse'.

The popularity of this new, fast and efficient way of travelling and transporting goods gradually saw a large part of the country connected up by a network of railways, which opened up remote parts of the country to western travellers and created a new industry. It also meant that the different castes were forced to share the same carriages and even to sit next to each other. In the 1840s Jamsetjee Jeejeebhoy and Dwarkanath Tagore were among the first Indians to set up their own railway companies, Tagore helping to raise capital for a service between Calcutta and the North-West and setting up the Great Western Bengal Railway Company in 1845. By 1880, there were 9,000 miles of track.

With the increased volume of travel came a variety of trains catering for specialised interests. One of the most famous and luxurious was the Palace on Wheels, with its lavishly decorated carriages – miniature copies of real palaces – attended by

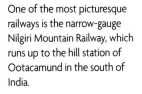

One of the most picturesque railways is the narrow-gauge Nilgiri Mountain Railway, which runs up to the hill station of Ootacamund in the south of India.

The *Fairy Queen Express*, the world's oldest locomotive still in operation.

personalised valets. The Life-Line Express, known as the Hospital on Wheels, was to provide healthcare in rural areas by means of carriages converted into operating theatres and recovery wards. In recent years double-decker carriages have been introduced, as well as women-only carriages. There are special trains for pilgrims – effectively hotels on wheels with a cook and a doctor on board – pilgrimage being a very common reason for travelling in India.

Perhaps the most picturesque railway of all is the narrow-gauge Nilgiri Mountain Railway running up to the hill station of Ootacamund in the south of India, and connecting important and interesting hill resorts through rugged and scenic mountain landscapes. As the oldest and steepest example of 'rack and pinion' technology (which enables the locomotive to ascend precipitous gradients), it is nowadays considered an 'outstanding example of the interchange of values in technology', and designated a world heritage site. Such hill-station railways functioned as a phased colonisation of the hills by the British, especially for military garrisons. The first of these hill stations was Simla in the north, later becoming the summer capital of the Viceroys. Another, Darjeeling was home to the world-famous emerald tea garden, with its narrow-gauge railway built between 1879 and 1881, now a world heritage site. All three lines are now popular tourist destinations for western travellers and railway enthusiasts.

The oldest operating locomotive in the world is India's *Fairy Queen Express*, while the longest railway platform, at 4,483 feet, is also in India, at Gorakhpur. Bombay's railway station was named after Queen Victoria on the day of her Golden Jubilee in 1887; the Victoria Terminus saw India's first electric railway trains introduced in 1925.

During the First World War, railway production in India was reduced to meet the demands of the British forces outside India. In the Second World War, too, locomotives and track materials were removed from India for the campaign in the Middle East, leaving the entire railway system in poor shape until after the war.

At the time of Indian Independence in 1947, there were 42 separate railway systems in the country, including 32 owned by the Indian princely states. Today there are 71,000 miles of rail track in India, carrying more than 23 million passengers daily and serving 7,112 railway stations. The Indian state-owned enterprise is operated by the Ministry of Railways and is the fourth largest rail network in the world.

Were the British Empire to disappear, it's works in India would remain one of the lasting monuments.

Otto von Bismark (1815–98), the first Chancellor of Germany

One of the first air mail letters.

World's first airmail letter

It was in India that the world's first official Aerial Postal Service took place on 18 February 1911 in a British-built Humber-Sommer biplane. The French pilot Henri Pequet took off from the grounds of the United Provinces Exhibition at Allahabad, with one sack of 931 registered items, to be delivered to the Official of the Indian Post Office at Naini Junction, a journey of 13 minutes, five miles away. The majority of them carried the cachet 'R/ALLAHABAD' stamped in black. The take-off of the historic flight was seen by more than a million people.

The man behind the whole idea was aviator pioneer Captain Walter George Windham who was invited in 1910 to take the flying machines from England to the big event at Allahabad. It was also the first time a plane flew in India. The Chaplain of the Holy Trinity Church of Allahabad asked Captain Windham if he could help him raise funds to build a hostel for Indian students under his care. The Captain, by way of wanting to boost the cause of aviation, thought of arranging an aerial postal service to do just that. He obtained permission from the Indian Post Office who would not sanction a charge over and above the normal postage rate, but asked for a nominal sum of six annas (sixpence) as a donation. The Chaplain was appointed as postmaster and people were asked to send stamped addressed envelopes to him. A special post mark, 4cm in diameter was also authorised in two colours, magenta for public mail and black for privileged items.

In 1961, the Indian Post Office issued three commemorative stamps to mark the Golden Jubilee of the first official airmail, Allahabad-Naini flight. Another set of two special stamps was issued in 1986 to mark the 75th anniversary of the historic flight.

CHAPTER 10
Notable Indians in Britain

The first Indian to come to England

For all his historical significance, it is incredible that the identity of the young man brought to England by the East India Company on 19 August 1614 should remain unknown. Indeed, other than that he was supposed to have been born in the 'Bay of Bengal', it is not even known what part of India his parents came from. But he has the distinction of being officially the very first Indian to have come to Britain.

Apparently this young Indian was 'given' to Thomas Best, the Captain of an East India Company ship, in March 1612 by the Commander of a Dutch ship on its way to Burma. He was put under the care of the Company preacher, Patrick Copeland, who taught him Latin, English and Christianity, at a cost to the Company of: '20 markes annually'. The Company therefore resolved, *'to have him kept here to school to bee taught and enstructed in religion that hereafter being well grounded he might upon occasion bee sent unto his country where God me bee soe pleased to make him an instrument in converting some of his nation...'*

'Peter's' baptism on 22 December 1616 at St Dionis Backchurch, London.

Well satisfied with his pupil's learning progress, Copeland wrote to the Court in 1615 of *'how much the Indian youth, recommended to his care, had profited in the knowledge of the Christian religion, so that he is able to render an account of his faith.'* He suggested that the young man be baptised, *'being of the opinion that it were fit to have it publicly effected, being the first fruits of India.'* The proposal was put to the Deputy Governor of the Company, Maurice Abbot, with a request that he mention it to his brother, George, the Archbishop of Canterbury, the Company being *'desirous to understand his opinion before they resolve anything in so weighty a business.'* The idea was welcomed by the Archbishop, and the young Indian was baptised on 22 December 1616 at St Dionis Backchurch (long since demolished) in Fenchurch Street in the City of London. Dr John Wood of Great St Helen's officiated, and the name 'Peter' given in baptism was chosen personally by King James I. The official record reads, 'An East Indian was christened by the name of 'Peter'.

Among the distinguished congregation were some of the members of the Privy Council, the Lord Mayor, Sir John Leman, and members of the East India Company and its sister Company of Virginia. The church was packed, and there was an immense crowd outside. A few weeks after the christening ceremony, accompanied by Chaplain Copeland, 'Peter' returned to India, 'to convert some of his own nation',

Majority of The East India Company boats that transported cargo and passengers between India and England were hired. They carried spices, gold bullion, coins, and manufactured items. During 233 years of trading, nearly 200 ships were lost, with inestimable losses to the traders.

Mirza Sheikh I'tesamuddin was the first Indian to document his experiences in the western world.

according to the records of the minute. Unfortunately, there is no further information about what happened to 'Peter Pope', as he came to be known. What he did in India is as much a mystery as to who he really was, or even his real name.

A few years later, in a sermon, Chaplain Copeland gave an account of his teaching success with 'Peter':

'I taught him (I not being able to speak otherwise to him, nor he to me, but by signs) to speak, to read and write the English tongue and hand, both Roman and Secretary, within less than the space of a year, so that his Majesty and many of the Nobility wondered at his handwriting; and within the compass of three years, I taught him the grounds of Religion, and to learn most of St Paul's Epistles by heart.'

According to some Indian Christian historians, the baptism of 'Peter' was a triumph of God's grace. For some academics, the baptism had 'symbolic protocolonial significance'. What is beyond doubt or argument is that, though by no means the first Indian to come to England, 'Peter' was the first to have been officially put on record and formally recognised by the King, the Church and the Privy Council, and as such made history that needs to be acknowledged and documented as an important episode in India's and Britain's shared heritage.

Early travellers in Europe

Regular traders from the East India Company also brought back Indians on their return to England. These were mostly men, sailors and servants whose names were not considered important enough to be registered on any documents. Among other early Indian arrivals to Europe were those who could bear their own expenses or be supported by well-wishers. Each one of these early visitors was an outstanding ambassador for India and aroused interest, curiosity and great respect wherever they went.

Mirza Sheikh I'tesamuddin (*c*.1730–1800) came to England in 1765 in the reign of King George III, with a mission to the British Court on behalf of the Emperor Shah Alam II. The mission was a failure, but he wrote a fascinating account in Persian of his travels in Europe and Britain. Translated by Kaiser Haq (2001), *The Wonders of Vilayet* is the first book about an Indian's experiences and observations of the western world. Historically a document of great interest, it is also written with humour and clarity. What makes this record of travels unique and enchanting is its description of Western culture, politics, religion, education, entertainment, the judiciary etc. and comparison of them with their Indian counterparts; it is an eighteenth-century view of East and West as never written before. Smoking with hookahs is compared with smoking pipes; Oxford colleges are seen as madrassas; snow is likened to the coloured powder used in the Hindu Festival of Holi; contracted marriages through mutual consents are juxtaposed with arranged marriages; the rich agricultural land of England compared to the poor stony land of Indian farms; the education of rich English children with the plight of poor, deprived Indian children. The list is endless and impressive. 'If I were to describe all the inventions made in England,' reflects I'tesamuddin with regret, 'I would need a very long life and many books to fill.'

Sake Dean Mahomed (1759–1851) came to England in 1807 after living in India and Ireland. He is the most notable early Indian to have made a name for himself in England as a writer, as a restaurateur and as a practitioner of alternative medicine. His book, *The Travels of Dean Mahomed*, published in 1794, is the first book written by an Indian in English. Part autobiographical, part historical and part travelogue, the book is about his early life in India, the domination of British rule in India, and his journey to Ireland. Britain's first Indian restaurant, the Hindoostanee Coffee House, was opened by Dean Mahomed in London in 1810. It did not do as well as he had hoped, and closed in 1812. Undaunted, he opened Mahomed's Baths in Brighton in 1814, treating patients suffering from muscular pain with *Champi* (shampoo – a form of massage) and vapour baths of aromatic oils and herbs. It was a great success, enjoying the patronage of King George IV, King William IV and Sir Robert Peel. In 1822 Mahomed published *Shampooing, or Benefits Resulting from the Use of Indian Medicated Vapour Bath*.

Sake Dean Mahomed one of the first Indian entrepeneurs in Britain and the bath house he opened in Brighton.

Statue of Raja Ram Mohan Roy in Bristol city centre. Unveiled in 1997, the year of India's Golden Jubilee.

Sir Jamsetjee Jeejeebhoy.

Raja Ram Mohan Roy (1772–1833) is renowned as the prophet of modern India and the greatest Indian of his time. A major figure in the Hindu reawakening of the 19th century, Roy was a dedicated social reformer and a scholar of world reputation in the disciplines of religion, literature and languages. He had a special concern for the poor and educationally deprived. He believed strongly in the freedom of the press and fought against the Press Regulation Act of 1823.

Pre-eminent among Roy's humanitarian reforms has to be his tireless fight for the abolition of *suttee*. Traumatised by the sight of his brother's widow on the funeral pyre, he campaigned against this inhuman custom in the press and on public platforms. When his opponents put up a petition before the Privy Council, Roy put forward a counter-petition before Parliament and won, finally in 1829, establishing the illegality of *suttee* and the right of widows to remarry.

In 1831 Roy was the first Indian to come to England on an official visit, bestowed with the title of Raja by the Moghul Emperor Shah Akbar II (1759–1837) as an honorary mark of respect. He was also the first Indian to be consulted by the British Parliament, presenting complaints on behalf of the Moghul Emperor against the Board of Directors of the East India Company. Though unfamiliar with England, Roy was no stranger to the English way of life: his knowledge of the English language and literature helped him understand the country's customs and culture. In London he attended parliamentary debates, especially those devoted to the Reform Bill and the abolition of slavery. His visit was a great success and, impressed by his arguments, the directors of the East India Company revised its charter in order to accelerate the promotion of Indians in its institutions.

Politically, like the Moderates, Raja Ram Mohan Roy was against full independence of India, arguing that British rule in India was a 'divine dispensation' and favouring the movement towards the country gaining gradual control of its administration. Fundamentally, he believed, the English presence in India would benefit the people of India, and 'India would remain India,' he asserted, 'no matter what the influence of the West: its history and culture were immutable'.

The Raja died in 1833, and is buried in Arnos Vale cemetery in Bristol.

Sir Jamsetjee Jeejeebhoy (1783–1859), merchant and philanthropist, was the first Indian to be knighted, and in 1859 the first Indian to be created a hereditary Baronet by Queen Victoria. His first business venture was collecting and selling empty bottles, which earned him the nickname the 'Bottlewalla', dealer in bottles. The period of European imperialism in India enabled him to become a successful businessman exporting cotton and opium, making him rich enough to buy his own fleet of ships to supply European, Chinese and American traders. As the most prominent Indian merchant he also became the chief representative of the Indian community, in 1843 being made the only Indian director of the Bombay Bank.

A great philanthropist, Jeejeebhoy established schools and hospitals in co-operation with the British, building the J J School of Art and the J J Hospital, and was responsible for constructing bridges, waterworks, causeways and reservoirs all over India. His loyalty to the British and his humanitarian work brought him honours; at the time he was the most famous Indian, as well as the first non-European colonial subject. In 1860 an act was passed stipulating that each holder of the baronetcy must relinquish his own name to take that of the first holder of the title: Baronet Jamsetjee Jeejeebhoy.

Ardaseer Cursetjee (Wadia) (1808–77), was an Indian shipbuilder and engineer who has the distinction of being the first Indian to be elected Fellow of the Royal Society, in 1841, having been nominated by its President as 'a gentleman well versed in the theory and practice of naval architecture and devoted to scientific pursuits'. He is credited with the introduction of gas lighting in Bombay as well as having built a sea-going vessel of 60 tonnes which he adapted as a steam engine. He introduced the sewing machine, photography and electroplating to India. He was invited to the wedding of Queen Victoria to Prince Albert in 1840.

Ardaseer Cursetjee.

Maharaja Duleep Singh (1838–93), son of the famous Maharaja Ranjit Singh, the 'Lion of Punjab', was the last Maharaja of the Sikh Empire and a victim of the Anglo-Sikh wars. After the death of his father and the annexation of Punjab by the East India Company in 1849, the British assumed his guardianship, confiscating the state's property and its famous Koh-i-Noor diamond in return for granting him a pension. His conversion to Christianity as a minor in 1853, though approved by the Governor-General Lord Dalhousie, remains debatable. But as a matter of British policy, he was to be anglicised in every possible respect.

In 1854, the East India Company allowed Duleep Singh to come to England where, after a short stay in a hotel in London, the Company found him more permanent accommodation and an annual pension. Eventually the India Office purchased for him a country estate at Elveden in Suffolk.

Maharaja Duleep Singh.

Duleep Singh transformed the run-down house into a semi-Indian palace, where he lived the life of a British aristocrat entertaining the gentry and the Prince of Wales. When first presented to the Court, he was received with special consideration by Queen Victoria and Prince Albert. The Prince of Wales and his brothers and sisters treated him with great friendliness, and he was often invited to stay with the Royal Family at Osborne House. When the Koh-i-Noor diamond was shown to him, he said gallantly that it gave him great satisfaction to hand it in person to the Queen.

As a result of his extravagant lifestyle, Duleep Singh got into financial difficulties that soon made him a tireless and troublesome suitor at the India Office. In the end he had to give up Elveden Hall and there were no more shooting parties. He even demanded the Koh-i-Noor diamond back and accused the Queen of being 'Mrs Fagin'.

Disheartened and in 'exile', the Maharaja started learning about Sikhism and, in 1886, decided to return to India, with the intention of reclaiming his position as the

Sir John Spencer Login, Scottish surgeon, went to India in 1832. In 1849 he became guardian of the 10-year old Duleep Singh and the Koh-I-Noor diamond.

Syed Amir Ali.

head of the Sikh people. In the face of the British Government's opposition, he set sail for 'home', but sadly the voyage was intercepted at Aden and he was arrested and brought back to Europe.

As a last resort, he considered placing his services as the King of Punjab at the disposal of Russia, but the Czar refused the offer. Disillusioned, he went to live in Paris, where he died in 1893. He is buried in St Andrew & St Patrick's Church, Elveden.

Syed Amir Ali (1849–1928), author and jurist, was the first Muslim to graduate from Calcutta University. He came to Britain on a scholarship in 1870, joined the Inner Temple, and in 1873 was called to the Bar, the first Muslim to do so. Ali also became the first Muslim Judge at the Calcutta High Court and in 1911 was instrumental in setting up the Red Crescent Society, the Muslim 'Red Cross'. He was made an honorary LLD of Cambridge University and in 1909 became the first Indian to be appointed to the Privy Council.

When Cornelia Sorabji, the first woman to practise law in England and India, wrote a letter to *The Times* on 26 September 1902 pointing out how legally disadvantaged women were while in purdah (the *purdahnishins*), and suggesting the appointment of female lawyers to help them, Syed Amir Ali supported her. 'A post like the one you suggest,' he wrote to her, 'would afford, in my opinion, great help to these poor women and be of assistance to the Government in acquainting itself with the wants, needs and requirements of *purdahnishin* ladies.' *The Times*'s editorial of 11 October 1902 responded to his letter by quoting *The Queen* magazine's praise for 'Mr Justice Ameer Ali', for succinctly putting the case both on the evil and its cure. On Syed Ali's advice, Cornelia decided to take a job at a solicitor's office in India.

Pandita Ramabai Saraswati.

Pandita Ramabai Saraswati (1858–1922) was orphaned in childhood and widowed in her youth which made her unwelcome in the community. To fight the ills and prejudices of society, she embarked on a mission for the emancipation of women. She learnt Sanskrit and went on a lecture tour of India to promote the founding of shelters for widows and the socially outcast. Ramabai then learned English and came to England in 1883 for further studies, staying with the Sanskrit Scholar at Oxford, Max Müller. While in England, she converted to Christianity and took up a two-year professorship at Cheltenham Ladies College before travelling to America.

On her return to India in 1889, Pandita Ramabai opened her first home for widows, offering teaching and nursing courses in order to make them economically independent. India issued a commemorative stamp in her honour in 1989 to mark the centenary of the opening of the first home for the widows.

Kadambini Ganguli (1861–1923) was the first Indian woman to qualify as a doctor in 1886, trained in English medicine at the Calcutta Medical College. Before that, she had already received her BA in 1882 from Bethune College of Calcutta University.

After qualifying, she set up her own private medical practice. In 1892, Dwarkanath Tagore sponsored her to travel to Britain for further studies, at the time, one of the few Indian women to do so. Kadambini gained post-graduate qualifications in medicine and surgery from Edinburgh, Glasgow and Dublin, eventually retuning to India and opening her own medical practice. She was the midwife when Satyajit Ray, the great Indian film director was born.

Politically very active, Kadambini was a great supporter of female suffrage and was the first woman to address the open session of the Indian National Congress in 1890. In 1906, she organised the Women's Conference in the aftermath of the partition of Bengal.

Rabindranath Tagore (1861–1941), author of *Gitanjali* and its 'profoundly sensitive, fresh and beautiful' verse became the first non-European to win the Nobel Prize for Literature, in 1913. On a visit to London in 1912, Tagore had left his briefcase containing the manuscript of the English translation of *Gitanjali* on an underground train while travelling between Charing Cross and Russell Square. Luckily, it was recovered from the lost property office the following morning.

At the age of seven, Tagore went to school in Brighton. He later studied at London University, attending Henry Morley's lectures in English Literature and Shakespeare, and often visited the House of Commons to listen to the debates. In London he was lucky to find accommodation with an English family, though the family's two daughters, taken aback at the presence of a 'blackie', left home.

Tagore was received at Queen Victoria's court and hailed as a poet who brought

Far left: Rabindranath Tagore.

Left: Kadambini Ganguli.

Right: Cornelia Sorabji.

Far right: Baroness Hale of Richmond, President of the Supreme Court of the United Kingdom, unveiling the bust of Cornelia Sorabji in 2012. Copies of the bust, donated by the author, are now displayed at the Supreme Court and the Honourable Society of the Lincoln's Inn, London.

'the East to the West'. He was knighted in 1915 but renounced the honour after the Jallianwalla Bagh massacre in 1919. In 2011 a bust of Tagore was unveiled by Prince Charles in London's Gordon Square.

Cornelia Sorabji (1866–1954) Social reformer and barrister, holds a very special and prominent position in the history of India's pioneering women. Quite simply, she was one of a group of outstanding women of her time whose dedication to public service sustained them throughout their lives, and whose courageous efforts and achievement brought them celebrity status and an honoured place in history. A defender and reformer of the legal status of women and children in India, Cornelia described this era as the 'Age of the Individual'. She was a prolific writer, and her voluminous diaries and letters – she is to letters what Samuel Pepys is to diaries – are also a record of her life in India and Britain.

Cornelia was the first, and only, female to study at the Deccan College in Poona in 1884, and the first girl-graduate of western India. Despite being a brilliant student she was denied a scholarship to a British university, a privilege reserved for men only. An alternative scholarship, funded by her well-wishers in Britain, including Florence Nightingale, enabled her to go to Somerville College, Oxford in 1889, where she was the first ever woman to study law. She had to be chaperoned to her lectures and have special permission to take the Bachelor of Civil Law examination in 1892. She was also the first female to use the Codrington Library at All Souls.

At Oxford, Cornelia had the good fortune of meeting Benjamin Jowett, the Master of Balliol College, who 'adopted' her and introduced her to many eminent individuals, including Gladstone, Balfour, Asquith, Max Müller and George Bernard

Shaw. After a legal training in London, Cornelia returned to India in 1894 and found a niche working for the *purdahnishins* (women in purdah) who in the absence of female legal advisers regularly suffered injustice in matters of their inheritance. Cornelia, as a woman was barred registering as a lawyer, but took LLB and pleaders examinations to help these women and minors with property cases under the Court of Wards, becoming the first woman to do so. Her pioneering work made her well known; it is estimated that she helped more than 600 women and children annually.

The legal profession was closed to women until 1919: Cornelia was 57 before she was called to the Bar at Lincoln's Inn in 1923 and only then awarded her degree for the Bachelor of Civil Law examination she had taken 30 years earlier. In 1924, she was enrolled as an Advocate of the Calcutta High Court and joined the Northern Circuit in England. She organised the National Council of Women in India and in 1929 was appointed by the Government the Hon. Member, Labour Commission (India).

Over the years Cornelia made many influential friends, among them Arnold Toynbee, T S Eliot, Dr Elizabeth Garrett Anderson and members of the British Royal Family, though her eminence attracted controversy outside the legal profession.

Invited by Princess Marie Louise to write a book for the library of Queen Mary's Doll's House, Cornelia created a story called *The Flute-player's Dolls*.

Cornelia was an Indian whose loyalty to the British Raj never wavered. 'My heart beats with two pulses', she used to say: 'once for India and once for Britain'. Politically she favoured dominion status for India, as did the Moderates in India. She opposed Gandhi's demand for full independence and spoke at the Institute of Politics, Williamstown, USA, on British rule in India, condemning his campaign of civil disobedience and arguing for the law of the land to be upheld. In 1931, she interviewed Gandhi when he was in London for the Second Round Table Conference, in order to 'understand' him, but due to their differences of opinion, the encounter amounted to little more than an interrogation.

It is difficult to define Cornelia as either a feminist or an imperialist. She was both very English and very Indian, and her life spanned both cultures. In any event, no other Indian, male or female, had represented their mother country in Britain as Cornelia had: as a student, as a friend, as a lawyer and as an intellectual. With her intellect and knowledge she could have opted for an easy life in India; instead she chose the hard way – to fight for justice for women and children with enormous courage and integrity. She fulfilled her family motto: *We are in this world to serve others*.

The Right Honourable Sir Shadi Lal (1872–1945) made history when from 1934 until 1938 he served as a judge on the Judicial Committee of the Privy Council, the highest court of appeal in the Indian High Courts.

Lal studied at the Government College in Lahore in 1894 and came first in the examinations for the whole of Punjab, before going on to read law at Oxford. In 1920 he was the first Indian to be appointed Chief Justice of any High Court in India

The Rt Hon Sir Shadi Lal.

when he took over as the Chief Justice of the Lahore Court, holding the position for 14 years. A photograph of this authoritative lawyer and great Indian luminary, now adorns the main corridor of the Supreme Court of the United Kingdom.

Keshub Chandra Sen.

Keshub Chandra Sen (1838–84) philosopher, social reformer and educator, founded the Brahmo Samaj of India and was the secretary of the Asiatic Society in 1854. He visited England for six months in 1870 to give a series of 60 lectures, and met William Gladstone and other parliamentarians. Often speaking twice a day to packed audiences, he talked about religion, philosophy, female education and especially about an Alliance with Britain and Britain's duty to India. Before returning to India, Sen had an audience with Queen Victoria at Osborne House, where the Queen presented him with a large engraving of herself and two books personally signed, 'To Babu Keshub Chandra Sen, from Victoria RG, September 1870.

Mohammed Ali Jinnah.

Mohammed Ali Jinnah (1876–1948) came to England in 1893 and studied at Lincoln's Inn, in 1896 becoming the youngest ever student to be accepted at the Bar. He was a frequent visitor to the House of Commons to see the workings of the powerful British Government. Returning to India, he practised law in Bombay, while pursuing his interest in politics by representing Bombay's Muslims on the Imperial Legislative Council and later by joining the Muslim League. For a while he took the lead in trying to unite Hindus and Muslims. Jinnah opposed the non-cooperation policy of the Indian National Congress, and resigned from it in 1920. After his visit to England for the Second Round Table Conference in 1931 he went back to India to devote his time to the Muslim League and demand a separate state for Muslims. For his instrumental role in the creation of the nation of Pakistan in 1947, of which he was the first Governor-General, he is acclaimed for having genuinely changed the destiny of Muslims.

Srinivasa Ramanujan.

Srinivasa Ramanujan (1887–1920), a child prodigy who despite virtually no formal education in pure maths, made amazing contributions to mathematical analyses, number theory, the theories of infinite series and continued fractions. A self-taught genius, he attracted the attention of a mathematician who passed his work on to Cambridge University. A correspondence ensued with the brilliant Cambridge mathematics professor G H Hardy, who in 1914 invited Ramanujan to Trinity College.

At Cambridge, Ramanujan produced over 20 research papers in collaboration with other prominent mathematicians like Hardy, and in 1916 he was awarded a BA degree and in 1918 was elected a Fellow of the Royal Society. An international publication, the *Ramanujan Journal*, was launched to publicise all areas of mathematics influenced by him. In recognition of his work, the Government of India declared his birthday, 22 December, Mathematics Day. Ramanujan died very young, but his work was studied by eminent mathematicians of the Atomic Energy Commission and the TATA Institute of Fundamental Research of India.

Princess Sophia (1876–1948) was the daughter of Maharaja Duleep Singh and god-daughter of Queen Victoria. Putting aside her royal status and pampered existence, she lived the life of an ordinary person in Britain fighting for equality and voting rights for women, becoming one of the most active Indian members of the suffragette movement under Emmeline Pankhurst. She took part in protest rallies around the country and distributed pamphlets outside public buildings, and joined the Women's Tax Resistance League which was linked to the Women's Freedom Movement. In 1910 she took part in the famous disturbance at Caxton Hall in London, known as 'Black Friday', which was also attended by Emmeline Pankhurst, where there were ugly clashes between the police and the suffragettes. In 1928, after Pankhurst's death, she became the President of the Committee of the Suffragettes Fellowship.

Princess Sophia's entry in *Who's Who* for 1934 quotes her as describing her purpose in life as 'the advancement of women', an aspiration her very influential role in the suffragette movement certainly proved. Her great disappointment was that, no matter what law she broke or how serious the offence, her royal status prevented her from being imprisoned.

Though she never lived in India, the Princess was also interested in fighting for similar rights for women in India. Her profound interest in India's politics saw her make contact with national leaders and freedom fighters like Gokhale, Tilak and Lajpat Rai.

During the First World War Princess Sophia worked as a nurse and visited various

Below left: Princess Sophia Duleep Singh selling *The Suffragette*, 1913.

Below: The India section of the 1911 'Coronation Procession', believed to show Mrs PL 'Lolita' Roy and her 3 daughters.

Printed tiles of Princess Sophia Duleep Singh (left) and Lolita Roy (centre) which are included on the plinth (right) of the statue commemorating Millicent Fawcett and the suffragette movement in Parliament Square, London. The first Indian women to be recognised in such a distinguished setting.

Aga Khan III, Sir Sultan Mohamed.

hospitals where Indian soldiers were recovering from their wounds. Twenty-one years later, another Princess, also from Punjab, Princess Indira of Kapurthala (1912–79), followed Princess Sophia in caring for the wounded in the Second World War.

Lolita Roy (c.1865 – unknown), who came to England from India in 1901, was an advocate of female suffrage both in India and in Britain, fighting for women's freedom and the right to vote. Indian Suffragettes benefited greatly from her leadership and influence within the main movement, although women in India had to wait until Independence in 1947 before they were given the right to vote.

As President of the London Indian Union Society, and with the support of Women's Social and Political Union (WSPU), she organised a number of fundraising events for Indian women's education and training in Britain.

Celebrating the Coronation of King George V in 1911, Lolita led the Women's Coronation Procession in London, flying the elephant emblem of India. She is also remembered on a statue in Parliament Square, London for her influential role in the Women's Suffrage Movement.

The **Aga Khan III, Sir Sultan Mohamed** (1877–1957), a descendant of the Prophet Mohammed, was the 48th hereditary spiritual leader of the Khoja Islamists. He first came to England in 1898, and had an audience with Queen Victoria at Windsor Castle, and the honour of being seated next to her at state banquets. His wealth and experience gave him a commanding position as a diplomat and in his friendship with the British Royal Family. In 1920 the Aga Khan led the Indian delegation to Geneva to attend the Disarmament Conference.

In 1930 and 1931 he was a member of the Round Table Conferences in London, and seen as a friend of the British people, often meeting Sir William Wedderburn, with a view to improving relations between India and Britain. In India he was one of the founders, and the first president of the All-India Muslim League to protect Muslim rights in India. He was made a member of the Royal Privy Council in 1934.

Mithan Ardershir Tata (1898–1981) was the first Indian woman barrister, called to the Bar in London at the Honourable Society of the Lincoln's Inn in January 1923. She was also the first woman lawyer at Bombay High Court. A BA graduate of Bombay University, Mithan came to London in 1919 to give evidence to the Royal Commission on Indian Reforms at the House of Commons. She gave talks at various public meetings about female suffrage in India and was a guest speaker at Women's Freedom League in London, on the subject of 'Indian women and the vote' and travelled to Scotland to speak on the subject of female franchise in India.

On her return to India, Mithan edited *Stri Dharma*, the journal of the All India Women's Conference and published her autobiography, *Autumn Leaves*.

Vikram Sarabhai (1919–71) scion of a famous Sarabhai family from Ahmedabad, was a scientist and innovator, often regarded as the father of India's Space Programme. He studied at Cambridge obtaining a Doctorate on *Cosmic Ray Investigations in Tropical Latitudes*. He set up the Indian Institute of Management in Ahmedabad and was responsible for rocket launch stations in India. The establishment of the Indian Space Research Organisation was his greatest achievement.

An unique honour was bestowed upon him at a meeting of the International Astronomical Union which decided to name a moon crater after him, the 'Sarabhai Crater.'

Vikram Sarabhai was married to Mrinalini, professional Indian dancer, and sister of Lakshmi, Captain in the Indian National Army.

Far left: Mithan Ardershir Tata.

Left: Dr Vikram Sarabhai.

CHAPTER 11

India on Display

Exhibitions in Britain, 1798–1991

The first exhibition of Indian treasures in England in 1789, is only mentioned in catalogues. Unfortunately no detailed records survive, but the valuable exhibits, picked up or pillaged from India, were shipped to England by the East India Company, a sort of Colonial treasure hunt.

They were displayed at the Company's premises, East India House in Leadenhall Street, London, which was transformed into a museum.

The huge collection included exquisite ornaments, jade and ivory carvings, an ivory throne and bed, 16th and 17th century paintings of Indian landscapes, silk embroidery, figurines of gods and goddesses, a model of the Taj Mahal. There were also casts of details from Emperor Akbar's palace, carved panels from his tomb and part of his throne, along with a number of natural history specimens.

After the Mutiny of 1857, the East India Company ceased to exist and their premises were demolished in 1861. The India Museum was temporarily transferred to Fife

East India Company Museum,
Leadenhall Street.

Queen Victoria and Prince Albert viewing the Koh-i-Noor diamond in 1851. It was protected by an ornate metal cage. Any attempt to steal it triggered the metal base door to open and the diamond would drop inside an iron box below.

House on the banks of river Thames. In 1869 it was moved to the India Office which was by then anxious to get rid of the exhibits. The collection was relocated, in 1875, to rented rooms in the South Kensington Museum, now the V&A. Finally, in 1879, it was divided between The British Museum, the Natural History Museum and the Royal Botanic Gardens Kew, with a large section remaining at the V&A, including the famous tiger of Tipu Sultan.

During Queen Victoria's reign India was again put on display in a number of major exhibitions, each one showing the country in a most magnificent and exotic splendour which in turn, enhanced the glory of the Queen Empress.

One of the first, the Great Exhibition of 1851, organised at the suggestion of Prince Albert and described as 'alluring, imaginative and ambitious', was the most lavish of all, in depicting the outstanding success story of Britain in the 19th century. Exhibits came from Europe, the Middle East, China, Russia, Canada, West Africa and the Colonies.

The Indian section, the largest and most colourful, was also the most admired. Its exhibits, works of art and industry, were supplied by the East India Company for the 'mutual advantage of great importance both to India and Britain.' The *howdah* (a seat for riding on an elephant) was especially admired; it also caused the exhibition committee a great deal of difficulty, since they could not find a suitable stuffed elephant. In the end they borrowed one from the museum at Saffron Walden, but not without persuasion. The exhibit that stole the show was the 186-carat Koh-i-Noor diamond, confiscated from the Maharaja of Punjab and given to

Queen Victoria in 1850. The Queen herself visited the exhibition no less than 50 times with her children and visiting nobilities from abroad, and recorded every visit in detail in her journal:

June 16 1851: The whole of the Indian section beginning with the rare products – including the splendid jewels and shawls, embroideries, silver bedsteads, ivory chairs, models, is of immense interest and quite something new for the generality of people, these latter articles having hitherto only come over as presents to the Sovereign.

October 23 1851: To the Great Exhibition of the Works of all Nations and in particular to the Indian Section... The Jewels are truly magnificent. They had also belonged to Ranjit Singh and had been in the Treasury at Lahore. This one is the largest in the world therefore even more remarkable than the Koh-i-Noor! I am very happy that the British Crown will possess these jewels, for I shall certainly make them Crown Jewels.

The Colonial and Indian Exhibition of 1886, set up at the suggestion of the Prince of Wales, was another great success. It was furnished with beautiful models of P&O steamers, which plied the sea route to India, and featured parades of Indian soldiers who had fought shoulder to shoulder with British troops in Afghanistan, Egypt and Sudan. The greatest attractions of the exhibition were the hunting trophies, the peacocks, alligators and pythons. Other exhibits included richly coloured pottery, silkwork, paintings and carpets. No fewer than 3,000 specimens of timber were on display, as well as a model of an Indian fruit shop. Skilful artists sat at work in the palatial Durbar Hall.

The Indian contribution to the Glasgow Exhibition of 1888 was devoted to Indian artefacts from Bengal and Punjab and had an Indian confectionery shop.

These exhibitions represented the high noon of Victorian imperialism, and some of their exhibits are still on display in British museums and art galleries: the Jaipur Gate, for example, in the Hove Museum and Art Gallery; the ornate and magnificent Durbar Hall in Hastings Museum and Art Gallery and the teak gateway from the Maharaja of Jaipur is in the Horniman Museum in south London.

The great success of the Colonial and Indian Exhibition led the Prince of Wales to suggest the setting up of the new Imperial Institute, as a permanent monument to the 50th year of Queen Victoria's reign. It was paid for by all parts of the Empire and inaugurated by the Prince of Wales in 1893. The building, except for the central tower, was demolished in the 1950s and 1960s. The Imperial Institute later became the Commonwealth Institute in London's Holland Park, until finally closing in 2000. Some of its items were donated to the British Empire and Commonwealth Museum in Bristol, though this too is now no more.

At the Empire Timber Exhibition of 1920, and the Empire Exhibition of 1924, the beauty of certain woods from India generated huge excitement and as a result

The Indian Courtyard at the 1924 Empire Exhibition.

greatly increased their value. When India House, the High Commission, was built in 1930 at Aldwych, London, the architect Sir Herbert Baker, fitted and furnished the entire building using timber from India. The British Empire Exhibition was designed to demonstrate British power and achievements to the world. It was a colourful show of imperial might and opened by King George V and Queen Mary. The Indian section was modelled on the Jama Masjid in Delhi and the Taj Mahal. In 1926 the official caterer for the Indian Pavilion, Edward Palmer, opened Veeraswamy in London, now the oldest surviving Indian restaurant in Britain. Among its diners were Winston Churchill, Pandit Nehru, King Gustav of Sweden and Charlie Chaplin.

In 1984 Prince Charles wrote in his foreword to the book *India in Britain*, *'Today, 35 years after independence, India still has considerable influence on the life of Britain... with many people from the sub-continent determined to succeed in their various endeavours in the country of their adoption. There may be no more princes or Indian orderly officers, but the culture of India can still enrich and expand our lives in many different ways...'* 'Less well known,' added Indira Gandhi in her foreword to the same book, *'is the story of Indians in Britain – not only those who showed off their wealth but those who battled for large causes, intellectual and political'.*

The largest and most recent British exhibition exclusively about India, was held at the National Portrait Gallery in 1991. *The Raj: India and Britain 1600–1947*, curated by Professor C A Bayly, Reader in Indian History at Cambridge University. It still remains the most successful historical exhibition ever mounted at the gallery. Accompanying it was a magnificent 432-page catalogue charting the creation and projection of British images of Indians and their lives, and of Indian images of the British. Innumerable institutions and individuals, including the Queen, lent exhibits. Its fore-word examined a noble theme: the long relationship between the peoples of one of the greatest ancient civilizations of the East, largely Hindu but part Muslim, and the representatives of various western trading nations.

As bilateral trade grows between India and Britain in the areas of manufacturing, financial services and skill development, it is important that we increase awareness of the historical and cultural links between the two countries.

India House, opened on 8 July 1930 by King George V. The twelve medallions on the outer walls, representing the arms of each Indian province act as seals of authority and the building's identity. They are also repeated on the marble floor of the entrance hall, under the dome. To enter the building is to set foot on Indian territory. All the wood and some of the stone work came from India. Inside, the walls and the ceiling are decorated with scenes from ancient Indian history, creating an atmosphere that is as fascinating as it is beautiful. Watercolour by Malcolm Sowersby.

Motoring in the Raj –
India's love affair with the Rolls-Royce

by John Fasal, author and publisher

At the dawn of motoring, it was the distinguished Parsee master of Anglo-Indian commerce, Sir Jamsetjee Jeejeebhoy who took to motoring on a visit to London in August 1902.

The pioneering motorist Montague Grahame-White befriended H H The Maharaja of Cooch Behar and accepted an invitation to go to India, taking several automobiles, including Mors and Léon Bollée which were used by their Royal Highnesses, the Prince and Princess of Wales during their visit to Calcutta in 1905.

The 1903 Delhi Durbar was a landmark in establishing a keen following for motoring when Messrs. Turner, Hoare & Co. The Bombay engineers, had an exhibition of cars there. The entire stock of steam and petrol driven cars were sold and among those who bought them were the princes of Baroda, Bhavnagar, Bahawalpur, Bharatpur and Porbandar.

The first Rolls-Royce cars of modest 10hp. manufactured in Manchester appeared in the latter half of 1904. In the same year the Delhi to Bombay Trial was held, a distance of 880 miles. It was Mr S F Edge of the Napier Company who supplied a fleet of cars to the Nizam of Hyderabad, a serious competitor to the forthcoming Rolls-Royce market before the Great War. By November 1906 the great engineer perfected the 40/50 hp model which became 'The Silver Ghost' and affectionately known as 'The Best Car in the World'

It was a private owner, Frank Norbury, who took his car to be entered in the 620 miles trial from Bombay to Kolhapur in 1908. In winning its class, the publicity enhanced the reputation of Rolls-Royce in India and his car was purchased by H H The Maharaja Scindia of Gwalior.

The Viceroy, The Earl of Minto wrote to the Company praising his 1909 Barker landaulette after 7000 mile of trouble free motoring. Claud Johnson saw the importance of a Rolls Royce presence at the 1911 Delhi Durbar and eight identical landaulettes were ordered by the Government of India for this very splendid event for the King Emperor George V and Queen Mary.

The Maharaja of Patiala took a great interest in motoring and purchased 25 'Silver Ghosts'. The Company set up showrooms in Bombay, Calcutta and New Delhi. It must be remembered that Rolls-Royce Ltd. only supplied the running chassis and the coach work was undertaken by numerous local coach-builders including those in the major cities of India.

HRH The Duke of Edinburgh seated in the Maharaja of Bharatpur's (standing) 1925 Rolls Royce Windovers Cabriolet during a visit to India in 1965.

Maharana Arvind Singh Mewar of Udaipur, alongside his 1934 Rolls-Royce Phantom II Windovers Sedanca de Ville originally supplied to H H The Maharaja of Rajpipla.

John Fasal is author and publisher of The Rolls-Royce Twenty (1979), The Edwardian Rolls-Royce (1994) and publisher of The Rolls-Royce Wraith. At his Hertfordshire house he has built a Durbar Hall which was opened in 2012 by HRH the Duke of Gloucester.

Approximately 700 Rolls-Royce cars were supplied out of a pre-war production of 23,000 cars. Although small, India created a significant impact and prestige for the Company. The special requirements for hunting vehicles, the elaborate interiors for enclosed bodies with silver and Ivory fittings won wide publicity for future sales and the golden era was the 1920s. Following the general depression of the early 1930s, the sales of luxury cars declined and the Rolls-Royce passed their franchise to Allied Motors in 1931, the year R-R Ltd. took over Bentley motors.

The Maharaja of Mysore was the last of the big spenders and ordered 17 of these cars between 1946 and 1949, a glorious end around the time of Indian Independence.

CHAPTER 12
Indian Politicians at Westminster

It is not generally known that as early as the late 19th and early 20th centuries three Indians were elected to the House of Commons. Though few know their names or have heard of their achievements, their politics say as much about Indian society as about British society, and the precedent they set has immense significance for Indo-British relations. Their political convictions could not have been more different: the Liberal centralist Dadabhai Naoroji, the Conservative lawyer Sir Mancherjee Bhownagree and the radical, first Labour and then Communist, Shapurji Saklatvala. They may have made little impact on political history, but their enduring achievement lies in having been elected at all.

Lal Mohan Ghosh (1849–1909), barrister, orator and politician, was the first Indian to stand for parliament in 1885, as a Liberal for Deptford, losing by 367 votes. He tried again in the 1886 election and lost by 627. His election campaigns did not escape prejudice from the press, who labelled him 'a stranger to English civilisation and Christianity' and accused him of being an 'Indian Baboo'.

Born in Bengal, Ghosh came to England in 1869 to study law at Middle Temple and returned to Calcutta in 1873 to join the Bar. He later returned to England representing the British Indian Association to fight for the right of Indians to enter the Civil Service. In 1903 he was elected President of the Indian National Congress.

Dadabhai Naoroji (1825–1917) the Grand Old Man of India, made history in 1892 by becoming the first Indian to be elected to Parliament. Representing Finsbury Central, he won by the narrowest majority of 5 votes, saddling him with the nickname 'Mr Narrow Majority'. He entered Parliament to the great displeasure of the Prime Minister, Lord Salisbury, who called him 'black man', a racist taunt that did not pass without cautionary remarks from Queen Victoria. Gladstone, on the other hand, declared his 'great satisfaction' at the election of Lord Salisbury's 'black man', strongly believing that, 'If our ancestors had cared for the rights of other people, the British Empire would not have been made'. Support also came from Florence Nightingale.

Naoroji had come to England in 1855, as a partner in the first ever Indian business firm in the City of London, Cama & Co., but resigned shortly afterwards, refusing to have anything to do with the company's trade in opium. He became the first

Lal Mohan Ghosh.

Professor of Gujarati and Life Governor at University College, London and in 1890 was a founder member of the monthly journal, *India*, the official voice of the Indian National Congress and its British Committee.

Dadabhai Naoroji lived in England for nearly half a century, where he pursued the cause of India with determination. The icon of Indian nationalism, he represented the culture and spirit of India in England. Frequently returning to India he remained involved in the politics of both countries simultaneously. In 1885 he was one of the founders of the Indian National Congress, becoming its President in 1886, 1893 and 1906, and published *Poverty and Un-British Rule in India*. Naoroji refused a knighthood twice, and declined an honour from the Shah of Persia.

A painting of Naoroji is in the entrance to the Stranger's Gallery in Parliament, and reproduced in the official guide to the Palace of Westminster.

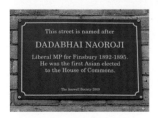

Above: Two plaques erected in memory of Naoroji, in the London Borough of Finsbury.

Above left: Dadabhai Naoroji.

Above: Baroness Boothroyd, the first female Speaker of the House of Commons, unveiling the bust of Dadabhai Naoroji at India House in February 1993 with His Excellency Dr L M Singhvi, (1931–2007) the Indian High Commissioner. The bust was donated by The Dadabhai

Naoroji Centenary Celebration Committee co-Chaired by Zerbanoo Gifford, Lady Maureen Thomas and Kusoom Vadgama to mark the historic election of Dadabhai Naoroji, the first Indian member of parliament at Westminster in 1892. The bust is now at the Nehru Centre, the cultural wing of the Indian High Commission.

Sir Mancherjee Merwanjee Bhownagree (1851–1933) came to England in 1882 to study law, and was called to the Bar at Lincoln's Inn in 1885. He stood for the parliamentary election of 1895 as a Conservative for the Bethnal Green constituency and won by 160 votes. He was re-elected in 1900 with a majority of 379, but failed in his third attempt in the 1906 election. Bhownagree inspired the House by the vigour and elegance of his speeches on Indian subjects and the rights of Indians in South Africa. Like Naoroji before him, he complained about the unjust drain of taxation on India and demanded India's economic independence, equal opportunity for Indian graduates and the raising of educational standards for women. He also argued the case for British investment in India in the field of technology, science and education. Bhownagree insisted that the government honour the pledge given by Queen Victoria to treat all her subjects equally and not let prejudice colour its dealings with the affairs of Indians.

Sir Mancherjee Merwanjee Bhownagree.

Bhownagree was a great organiser and negotiator both inside and outside politics. He was one of the Executives of the very successful Colonial and India Exhibition of 1886, which eventually evolved into the Imperial Institute, opened in 1893. He made a substantial contribution towards the building by funding the Bhownagree Corridor, named after his sister. He also donated a stained glass window at St Luke's Church in Radcliff Square, London in her memory, and in celebration of Queen Victoria's Diamond Jubilee in 1897 he commissioned a plinth in Bethnal Green Park.

In 1916 Bhownagree wrote *The Verdict of India* about the British in India and their positive influences, to counter German war propaganda about British treatment of the native population there. This was the period when even the hostile leaders of the Indian National Congress signed an address of loyalty and support for the war. Though in favour of British rule in India, Bhownagree nevertheless had reservations, and regretted that many of his aspirations remained unfulfilled.

Shapurji Saklatvala.

Shapurji Saklatvala (1874–1936) was the third Indian Member of Parliament for Battersea North, in 1922 for Labour and then in 1924 as a Communist. His oration in Parliament was notable for both its form and content. A passionate man who had witnessed the Indian contribution to the British war efforts during the First World War, he was incensed at the British government's ungenerous and brutal response in the aftermath of the conflict, especially in the case of the Jallianwalla Bagh massacre.

Saklatvala came to England in 1905 to study law. He joined the British Socialist Party and, impressed by the Russian revolution of 1917, became active in forming the People's Russian Information Bureau as well as the Communist Party of Great Britain. During the General Strike of 1926, he was imprisoned for making a fiery speech in Hyde Park. He was a strong critic of the Indian National Congress for their methods of fighting the British for independence. Saklatvala returned to India in 1927 but when he subsequently arrived back to Britain, his permit to re-enter India was cancelled at the request of the Indian Government.

Lord Sinha of Raipur.

Lord Sinha of Raipur KC (1863–1928) became the first and only Indian to be made a hereditary peer, in 1919. He was appointed permanent Advocate-General and member of the Viceroy's Council, and was the first Indian to 'take silk'. Jointly, with the Maharaja of Bikaner (1880–1943), Lord Sinha was appointed a member of the Imperial War Conference and the Imperial War Cabinet of 1917, and participated in the Peace Conference. He was also made a member of the War Ministry. He represented the India Office as Under-Secretary in the House of Lords and was appointed to the Privy Council, an honour earned by capability, earnest labour and gifted statesmanship. Lord Sinha personified all that was good in the co-operation between India and Britain.

Zerbanoo Gifford.

Zerbanoo Gifford (1950–) is the first Indian woman in history to stand for parliament, as the Liberal candidate for Hertsmere in 1983. Unfortunately she failed to win the seat, and tried again in 1987 and 1992, but without success. When elected to the Liberal Party's Federal Executive she became the first non-white person to be elected to any governing body of a British national political party; she was also a member of the Liberals' women's SDP Committee.

An author and human rights campaigner, Zerbanoo holds the International Woman of the Year Award 2006 for her humanitarian and charitable work. She was the Director of Anti-Slavery International, and is the Founding Director of the ASHA Centre in the Forest of Dean, which empowers young people from all over the world to be the leaders of tomorrow. She has been honoured by having a college named after her at the Dean Academy in Gloucester and is the first Indian woman to become a member of the Honourable Society of Knights of the Round Table.

Baroness Shreela Flather.

Baroness Shreela Flather (1934–) became the first Indian woman to be awarded a life peerage, in 1990, by Margaret Thatcher. She was Mayor of the Royal Borough of Windsor and Maidenhead and is a supporter of the British Humanist Association and an honorary associate of the National Secular Society and has been a board member of Marie Stopes UK for many years. She is an Honorary Doctor of Law, Leeds University, Honorary Doctor of the Open University and Northampton University, and a Fellow of University College, London.

Baroness Flather was recognised as the Asian of the Year in 1996 and was awarded the Pravasi Sanman, the Indian President's personal acknowledgement of overseas Indians.

CHAPTER 13
Indo-British Science

Construction site of the Koodankulam Nuclear Power Plant, 2009. (Photo: International Atomic Energy Agency).

When the East India Company went to India, they took with them their own doctors on board for the health and welfare of the crew as well as their staff in India. For the first time, English contemporary medicine was introduced in India where the ancient classical Ayurvedic (Hindu) and Unami (Muslim) were practised from earlier times. There was little or no knowledge of tropical diseases at the time.

As the British population increased in India, so did the demand for medical officers. The casualties of wars increased the need for medical attention and hospitals. One of the first hospitals was opened in 1679 at Madras followed by the Presidency General Hospital in Calcutta in 1796. Gradually a network of hospitals was set up in other major cities under the government of the Imperial India. Vaccination was introduced in 1902.

Alternative therapies – Yoga

For many years in Britain and across the world, yoga has been the most popular discipline of keeping mind and body in a healthy state. The 5000 years old Indian teaching of physical exercise as meditative and spiritual core was introduced to Britain and the West by Swami Vivekananda at his lectures at the Parliament of

Detail of a watercolour depicting Shiva seated in yogic postures, on a tiger skin, Murshidabad, late 18th century.

Religions at Chicago in 1893. Since then, it has been taught and practised as a complete exercise and physical therapy programme. Scientific studies have shown yoga's benefits on blood pressure, depression, chronic pain and anxiety, all without the use of conventional medicine. The United Nations General Assembly has marked 21 June as the International Yoga Day

Ayurveda

The treatment of illness by Ayurvedic method originated in India the same time as yoga. It is a complete healthcare system that treats physical ailments by focusing on yoga, massage, meditation, herbal medicine, acupuncture, breathing exercises and mantras. It is a wholistic approach to the mind, body and spirit with an aim to heal the patient rather than cure the disease.

A number of British physicians travelled to India to study Ayurveda and returned to open up their own practices and establish teaching institutes. There is a great public interest for a different kind of treatment for the cure of various illnesses, popularly known as 'alternative medicine' but is not without controversy about its effectiveness.

During the Raj, the practice of Ayurveda was restricted in favour of modern medicine. After Independence, Ayurveda has become part of the healthcare system with specially established centres across India.

Scientific Collaboration Between India and Britain

Professor Pankaj Vadgama, MB, BS, BSc, PhD, FRCPath, CChem, FRSC, CPhys, FInst, FIMMM, FRSB, CSci, Director of the Interdisciplinary Research Centre in Biomedical Materials Queen Mary University, London,

Science as an expression of cultural heritage on the part of both India and the UK has played an increasing role in the exchanges between the two countries. This has operated at the level of individual young researcher training programmes and visits through to major collaborative joint ventures. All of this represents a codifying of the many ongoing individual links over at least the last hundred years. India's ambitions were given form after independence; there was a high quality internal academic base but now harnessed increasingly to the needs of a new nation. One of the outcomes was the accretion of technical and research work within the network of extra-university research centres. The scale up has been accelerating, in line with the growing economy, and there are now 400 government funded laboratories and plans to establish completely new universities with world class stature. The Indian Institutes of Technology (IITs) have been a further individualistic expression of scientific prowess in India, their competitive intake of students, only 1% of applicants accepted, makes for a 'hot house' of quality education that has powered both Indian and overseas successes, most notably in silicon valley.

Within this changing landscape, UK – India research activity has become a true partnership in strategic areas. UK science policy has well recognised that the combination of societal need in a nation of 1.25bn coupled with a high quality scientific community can make for a step change both in the way research can be carried out and in the immediacy of societal benefit.

Multiple mechanisms have been set up, both by Government and by learned bodies in each country to firm up ties in strategic areas of science. The Indo-UK Science and Innovation Council is the government arm of the collaboration, and set up a range of collaborative platforms in 2014. The Newton–Bhabha Fund is the implementation route for this, and is designed to operate at multiple levels. There are Fellowships to enable research leaders to take ideas to the market place, together with a Programme on Industrial R&D collaboration, PhD placements in

UK/India through to joint research centres. Priorities for the latter include cancer biology, neuroscience, microbial resistance and renewable energy technology. A global health research programme on women and children's health has been delivered through the UK's MRC and India's Department of Biotechnology. A UK Royal Society managed programme for themed exchanges and meetings to catalyse academic collaboration right across the research spectrum has seen participation from over 80 institutions. A further key, multi-scale funding mechanism, combining education and research, has been the UK-India Education and Research Initiative (UKIERI) funded by the public and private sector, including the British Council and India's Department of Science and Technology (DST). Through mobility and integrated opportunities for innovation and skills a widening circle of collaboration has been secured. There have been over 25,000 research exchanges with 1,000 partnerships established. Critical mass can make a difference to the added value beyond any leveraging of individual capabilities, and example of this is a UKIERI multidisciplinary programme on fluidic devices for rapid, blood testing which benefits directly from the centralised microfabricaion resource available at an at a CSIR. The Newton Bhabha Fund is yet another funding opportunity for joint work, but here focussing on innovation to find solutions to development challenges. It includes amongst its priorities, sustainable cities, public health, high value manufacturing and big data.

The mechanisms for joint work no longer have to rely on eclectic individual effort; there are real underpinning strategies in place, agreed at the highest level. These are vital if joint work is to flourish to the benefit of both societies. Also, India has come of age scientifically and the old model for historically UK-based ties is no longer the basis for collaboration. In a global scientific world it is strictly business, if there is a special need for linkage because of a commonality of culture and history, it will need active effort in the face of increased competition for India's attention.

Indo-British Contributions in Science, Technology, Engineering and Medicine, 1614–2014

Professor Anthony D Dayan
LLB, MD, FRCP, FRCPATH, FFPM, FBTS

In the rich web of interaction in both directions in the 400 plus years of the scientific relationship between the two countries, some achievements have been so important that all humanity has benefited; others have been of more local benefit. Some have been appreciated at the time; others have had to wait for general understanding to catch up before being properly appreciated.

The following divisions between biosciences, science, engineering and technology are for convenience, but the boundaries are always fuzzy, as advances in one area may depend upon or lead to huge changes in another. There is a bias towards more recent leaders, as inclusion of many key historical figures would make the selection too long. There are many more people, just as important, who should be mentioned, but space is too limited for a comprehensive list.

Ronald Ross.

Chandrasekhara Venkata Raman.

Hargobind Khorana.

Venktraman Ramakrishnan.

Nobel Prize winners

Ronald Ross (1857–1932): 1902, Physiology or Medicine, for showing how malaria was transmitted.

Chandrasekhara Venkata Raman (1888–1970): 1930, Physics, whose analysis of light scattering led to deeper understanding of the behaviour and structure of proteins and other complex molecules.

Hargobind Khorana (1922–2011): 1968, Physiology or Medicine, who exposed the way in which the genetic code controlled protein synthesis.

Abdus Salam (1926–96): 1979, Physics, for a theory unifying different nuclear forces in quantum electrodynamics.

Subrahmanyan Chandrasekhar (1910–95): 1983, Physics, for explaining physical processes in the formation and evolution of stars.

Venktraman Ramakrishnan (1952–) 2009, Physiology or Medicine, co-explainer of how ribosomes synthesise proteins.

Biosciences (including Medicine)

The work in this field has deepened understanding of the mechanisms of health and disease in many biological systems.

Ananda Mohan Chakrabarty (1938–), pioneering genetic engineer whose US patent application underlay the debate over whether 'life forms' could be patented.

J B S Haldane (1892–1964), geneticist, Darwinian, writer and reluctantly repentant Marxist in Britain and India.

Frederick Henry Horatio Akbar Mahomed (c.1849–84), established the primary hypertension from that due to kidney disease; as a student devised a sphygmomanometer. His grandfather Sake Dean Mohamed opened the first Indian restaurant in Britain in 1810.

Autar Singh Paintal (1925–2004), pioneering neurophysiologist; recorded activity in single nerve fibres.

Jagadish Chandra Bose.

J B S Haldane.

Autar Singh Paintal.

Mankombu Sambasivan Swaminathan.

E P Reddy (1946–), biochemist who identified many oncogenic (cancer-causing) viruses and their effects on cells.

Krishnaswamy Vijay Raghavan FRS (1954–), explored how the nervous system and muscles develop.

Devi Prasad Shetty (1953–), heart surgeon and innovator of 'cheap and cheerful' cardiac surgery.

Mandyam Veerambudi Srinivasan (1948–), electronic engineer studying bee behaviour to explore ways in which the brain works.

Yellapragada Subbarao (1895–1948), biochemist who explored the energy sources in cells and treatment of cancer.

Mankombu Sambasivan Swaminathan (1925–), agricultural scientist. Introduced the 'Green Revolution' in India and is an international leader in scientific conservation.

Salim Ali (1896–1987), dedicated ornithologist and nature watcher.

Engineering and technology

Ajay Bhatt (1957–), co-developer of the USB (universal serial bus) for computers.

Sushanta Kumar Bhattacharyya (Baron Bhattacharyya, 1946–), expert on industrial manufacturing processes, notably in the automotive industry.

Kalpana Chawla (1962–2003), early astronaut. First Indian and third woman in space.

Ardaseer Cursetjee (Wadia) (1808–77), early engineer and constructor.

Vinod Dham (1950–), co-designer of the Pentium chip and of Flash memory.

William Lambton (1753–1823), Surveyor of India.

George Everest (1790–1866), Surveyor-General of India.

James Walker (1826–96), pioneers in the Great Trigonometric Survey of India, in which Mount Everest was first shown to be the highest peak in the world. They helped to found the Geological Survey of India, whose data have supported many advances in knowledge, from plate tectonics to national economic development.

Ajay Bhatt.

Kalpana Chawla.

Vinod Dham.

William Lambton.

Manali Kallat Vainu Bappu.   Homi J Bhabha.   Satyendra Nath Bose.   Meghnad Saha.

Ashok Amphora (1950–), pioneer in fluid dynamics at high pressures.

Raghunath Anant Mashelkar (1943–), advanced chemical engineer and worldwide educator.

Mysorean rockets (late 18th century), first effective rocket weapon used by Hyder Ali and Tipu Sultan against Arthur Wellesley in Mysore. Subsequently improved by Congreve.

Ratan Tata (1937–), engineer and industrialist.

T S Virdee (1952–), co-designer of the Large Hadron Collider at CERN.

Mokshagundam Vishweshvaraya (1860–1962), builder of cities, dams and other large public works.

Wootz steel, originated in India in the 3rd century BC: very hard, corrosion-resistant steel exported throughout Europe as 'Damascus' steel for weapons.

Science in academic and industrial organisations

Manali Kallat Vainu Bappu (1927–82), astronomer. Basic discoveries about stellar composition and evolution; founded modern astronomy in India.

Homi J Bhabha (1909–66), theoretical and practical nuclear scientist.

Shanti Swaroop Bhatnagar (1894–1955), physical chemist and scientific administrator.

Satyendra Nath Bose (1894–1974), quantum physicist; collaborator with Einstein.

Jagadish Chandra Bose (1858–1937), polymath, physicist, botanist and archaeologist.

Prasanta Chandra Mahalanobis (1893–1972), theoretical and applied public health statistician.

Meghnad Saha (1893–1956), astrophysicist who described the composition of stars; planner of major public works and founder of a technology institute.

Birbal Sahni (1891–1949), paleobotanist and geologist.

CHAPTER 14

Sport

With all the diversity of language, religion and caste the one thing that unites India as nothing else, is the love of sports and particularly cricket – closely followed by football, tennis, badminton, hockey, wrestling, motor sports, polo, snooker and chess – which has its origins in India, going back 1,500 years.

Polo

The game of polo is historically the oldest organised sport in the world, established by the Moghul Emperor Akbar the Great near Agra. No longer the 'game of kings', it was played in the hill villages of the North-West Frontier of India and taught to English cavalry officers and tea merchants. In 1859, the first polo club in India was founded in Silchar by Lieutenant Joe Shearer and Captain Robert Stewart. By the end of the 19th century, nearly all Indian and British army regiments were playing the game, including Lord Kitchener and Winston Churchill during their time in India.

Polo was introduced to England in 1869 by the Hussars, and the headquarters for the game established at The Hurlingham Club in London. India holds a very special place in the sport, which is often described as 'hockey on horseback'.

His Highness Prince Ranjitsinhji.

Cricket

After polo came the great imperial sport of cricket, and of all the bonds linking India and Britain, there is no harmonious example than the shared passion for cricket. It was introduced to India by the East India Company mariners in the first half of the 17th century, and the game was first played in India in 1721 by English sailors at Cambay. The Calcutta Cricket Club was founded in 1792 following the founding of the MCC at Lord's in 1787. The first Indian cricket team, the Parsee Club of Bombay, came to England in 1886, and again in 1888. For all their efforts, the only comment *The Times* newspaper could make was that 'Their cricket proved to be of the most elementary description'. It was not until 1911 that the next touring team came from India, captained by the Maharaja of Patiala and including the Gaekwad of Baroda, and not until the 1920s that India was granted full Test Match status. It was 1932 before the first Test match between India and England took place at Lord's, with England winning as they did again in 1936 and 1946, the last tour before Indian Independence. The period between 1890 and 1914 came to be seen as India's Golden Age, featuring many of the game's outstanding players, including the great Ranjitsinhji.

His Highness Prince Ranjitsinhji, later to become the Jam Saheb of Nawanagar in Gujarat (1872–1933), was the most famous and colourful Indian cricketer of his generation. Simply known as 'Ranji', he was the first Indian to play a Test Match for England, in 1893, and the first to make 3,000 runs in one season. A Cambridge blue and captain of Sussex, he scored 1,000 runs in each of the twelve full seasons he played, leading *Punch* magazine to give him the nickname 'Mr Run-Get-Singhji'. His career included a Test tour of Australia and a record 72 first class centuries. Playing for England against Australia at Old Trafford in 1896, 'Ranji' rescued his side after two shaky starts by scoring 62 and 154 not out. 'He may be the prince of India,' it was said, 'but he is the King of Cricket'. W G Grace (1848–1915), English cricket's greatest-ever player, declared that 'you will never see a batsman to beat him [Ranji] if you live a hundred years, who has put India on the map for the ordinary Englishman.'

During the First World War Ranjitsinhji led a contingent of Indian troops to the Western Front in 1914. He also made the full resources of his Gujarat State available to Britain, including his home at Staines which was converted into a hospital. Later the 'King of Cricket' served on the League of Nations, in 1929 prompting Lord Hailsham, then president of the MCC, to say, 'At least in the sphere of cricket, India has been granted Dominion Status if nothing else'.

Cricket is almost a religion in India, attracting vast crowds, the world's best international players and huge income from TV rights – and such is its popularity, especially with the new Twenty20 limited-over matches in the Indian Premier League – that India now generates more of world cricket's revenue than any other nation.

Sachin Tendulkar.

Cricket Match, 68th Light Infantry. This coloured print by P Carpentier shows a 68th Light Infantry team playing a cricket match in Calcutta on 15 January 1861 against the Calcutta Cricket Club.

Sachin Tendulkar (1973–) is widely regarded as the most prodigious batsman of modern times, and probably second only to Don Bradman as the greatest of all time. He made his Test debut in 1989 against Pakistan at 16, and went on to play for India, latterly as captain, for nearly 24 years. He is the only player to have scored one hundred international centuries, the first to score a double century in a one-day international, holds the record for the greatest number of runs in both Test cricket and one-day internationals, and is the only player to have scored more than 30,000 runs in international cricket. Besides his Test tours of England, Tendulkar also played for Yorkshire in the County Championship.

In 1997 Tendulkar received the Rajiv Gandhi Khel Ratna award, India's highest sporting honour. After his 200th, and final Test match, against the West Indies in Mumbai, in November 2013, he was awarded the Bharat Ratna, India's highest civilian award.

Kapil Dev.

Kapil Dev (1959–) made his cricket debut against Pakistan in 1978 as the greatest fast-bowling all rounder. He was voted India's Cricketer of the Century in 2002 and as Captain, led India to the 1983 World Cup. He was admired by his fans for his accuracy and ability to swing the ball as well as hit a ball brilliantly and with flair. Dev was the youngest player to reach 100 wickets and 1000 runs in Test Cricket.

Sunil Gavaskar (1949–) first played in a Test match against the West Indies in 1971 and has been regarded as one of the greatest opening batsmen of all time, winning admiration and respect, inside and outside the world of cricket. He set world records during his career for the most Test match runs and most Test centuries scored by any batsman and held the record of 34 Test Centuries for almost two decades until 2005. Gavaskar was also the first person to score centuries in both innings of a Test match thrice and widely admired for his technique against fast bowling.

Sunil Gavaskar.

CHAPTER 15

The Arts

Fine Art

Not content with written descriptions of the far-away land of spices, the English were given visual snapshots of India in landscape paintings. It was after the East India Company had become well established in India that in 1780 the landscape artist William Hodges became the first professional painter to go to India. Under the patronage of Warren Hastings he stayed there for six years, earning a great deal of money. A steady stream of his paintings powerfully conveyed the extent of India's panoramic beauty to the people of England, who hitherto had had no idea what India looked like. Now the East India Company's expansion created a market for colourful pictures both in India and in England; which were often reproduced in

Lakhota Palace, Jamnagar. The tower on the island in the centre of the lake is now a museum. There is a bronze statue of the cricketer Ranjitsinhji, the Jam Saheb of Jamnagar, in front of the tower.

Watercolour by Sir James Braithwaite Piele (1833–1906). He joined the Indian Civil Service in 1856 and was a British administrator for over 30 years. As a keen amateur artist he captured scenes of India under the Raj during his many travels.

The Taj Mahal, William Hodges, late 1780s.

black and white in English journals. The popularity of these hand-painted landscapes remained high until the arrival of the camera, which somewhat dented their appeal.

The acquisition of Indian territory offered many British residents a luxurious and comfortable way of life there. Reports of their wealth attracted further well-known and successful British artists to follow them to India, among them Arthur William Devis, Ozias Humphry, Tilly Kettle and Johan Zoffany, who mostly painted rich and powerful sitters, both British and Indian. In 1829 George Beeching went to Calcutta as the court painter and controller of the Moghul Household, and was given unprecedented access to the *zenana* (women's quarters) of the great Muslim Court in Lucknow to paint some of the ladies residing there. He always wore Indian clothes and, following Muslim tradition, had three wives.

Such paintings also revealed to a British audience the beauty of Indian architecture, with its influence soon being seen in British buildings like the Royal Pavilion at Brighton and Sezincote House in Gloucestershire, a notable example of Neo-Moghul architecture. Its admirers even took to employing Indian draughtsmen to design their mansions.

Uday Shankar.   Ram Gopal.

Dance

Uday Shankar (1900–77), the classical dancer and choreographer, reinterpreted folk and tribal dances as modern dance, earning him great popularity in the West. In 1931 he founded Europe's first Indian dance company which embarked on a seven-year world tour. Shankar was introduced to the Russian ballerina Anna Pavlova and together they performed the story of Radha and Krishna, with music by Comolata Banerji at the Royal Opera House in London. It caused a sensation, and their ensuing popularity took them to America and Mexico.

Ram Gopal (1912–2003) introduced the grace and beauty of Indian classical dance to the West. Performing mostly solo and touring Europe, he combined Indian dance with western ballet choreography. His first performance in London 1939 electrified the capital, and was even acknowledged by Queen Mary. In 1951 Gopal published *Indian Dancing*, and in 1962 opened a dance school in London, the Academy of Indian Dance and Music. In 1999 he was awarded the OBE.

Music

Ravi Shankar (1920–2012) was the best-known exponent of the sitar in the West, and brought Indian classical music to a new audience there. He began touring Europe and America in 1956, and his association with both the classical violinist Yehudi Menuhin and George Harrison of the Beatles, led him to write music for sitar in western orchestration. He also became the first Indian to compose music for western films. In 1958 Shankar participated in the celebrations for the tenth anniversary of the United Nations, and in the UNESCO music festival in Paris. Praised for his wonderful artistic imagination as well as for his technical mastery, Shankar gave performances that were detailed and precise, and among the most fascinating music heard by western audiences.

Freddie Mercury (1946–91), singer and song writer/lyricist of the rock band Queen, is perhaps the best-known Indian musician in the West. Born Farrokh Bulsara in Zanzibar, he grew up in India and came to Britain in 1963, where he attended the Ealing College of Art and became friends with several musicians. Eventually this led to the formation of Queen, a name he chose himself and the band released their first album in 1973. They are perhaps best known for *Bohemian Rhapsody*, a groundbreakingly long, epic, even operatic composition, that made Mercury an international star and a rock legend. His flamboyant personality and mesmerisingly theatrical live performances won him fans all over the world.

Ravi Shankar.

Cinema

Cinema first came to India in 1896 when agents for the pioneering film-makers the Lumière brothers showed a film in a hotel in Bombay. This led to foreign filmmakers coming to India to make documentaries. The first full-length Indian film was *Raja Harischandra* in 1912.

In 1941, during the Second World War, entertainment history was made. The first ever 'Indo-British' film, *The Court Dancer*, was released in India. A tale of doomed love between a courtesan and a prince, it starred the legendary Prithviraj Kapoor (1906–72), one of the doyens of Indian show business. Set in early 19th-century Manipur in north-east India, the costume drama was screened in English, but poorly dubbed into Hindi. Nonetheless, what was lost in language was made up for in music, dance and costumes.

Prithviraj Kapoor portrait 1929.

Today India is the largest film producer in the world, but it has not found equal success on the world stage. In the main, Indian-produced films are melodramatic and romantic, with irrelevant songs and dances and, worst of all, too long. The only two 'Indian' films to have made their mark internationally are *Gandhi* (1982), a very distorted sanitised view of his life, and *Slumdog Millionaire* (2008), both directed by Britons, Richard Attenborough (1923–2014) and Danny Boyle respectively.

One man who did break the mould of stereotypical Indian films was Satyajit Ray (1921–92), who directed no fewer than 36 films, the most famous being *Pather Panchali* and the *Apu Trilogy*. Much appreciated in the West, they won him international awards, as well as 32 Indian Film Awards and one Academy Award. In 2007 he was recognised by *Total Film* magazine as one of the greatest film directors ever.

Gurinder Chadha.

The one Indian woman who has broken through the glass ceiling and claimed the same stage as notable male film and theatre directors is Gurinder Chadha. Her films, *Bhaji on the Beach* and *Bend it Like Beckham*, have passed the British litmus test for proficiency; by showing that poking fun at one's self is a welcome sign of maturity she has captured the imagination of the third-generation Indians in Britain. TV dramas like *The Kumars at 42* and *Goodness Gracious Me* have also done exactly this with courage and confidence.

The 2002 film *Lagaan*, set in Imperial times, is the story of the people of a small village in Victorian India who stake their future on a game of cricket against their ruthless British rulers. The challenge is accepted and the game of cricket turns into a battle of wits against wickets. *Lagaan* received critical acclaim and became the third Indian film to be nominated for an Academy Award for Best Foreign Film after *Mother India* (1957) and *Salaam Bombay* (1988). Indian films of today are much influenced by the music, dance and culture of the West.

Literature

The impact of the English language on the ideas and ideals of the people of India was nothing less than a transformation of thought in the fields of law, literature and science. The early Indians of the 19th century writing in English – mostly men – are acknowledged for the intense patriotic passion of their writing; the noble Orientalists are admired for their pioneering work in discovering India's great intellectual heritage.

Bankim Chandra Chatterjee.

Bankim Chandra Chatterjee raised nationalism to the level of worship, and pleaded patriotism as the highest faith. He was regarded as a 'nation builder' and a major contributor to the making of modern India. Many believe the song he wrote, *Vande Mataram* (Hail to Mother), should have been chosen as the national anthem.

The study and publication of ancient Indian literature by the Asiatic Society of Bengal promoted the majesty of the Sanskrit language. Among the many dedicated to such work were Monier Monier-Williams (1819–99), a Sanskrit scholar, Henry Thomas Colebrooke (1765–1837), reknowned scholar, who translated major legal Sanskrit classics. Rajendralal Mitra (1823–91), an Indologist, was the first Indian President of the Asiatic Society and a pioneer in the scientific study of history. R G Bhandarkar (1837–1925) attended the International Conference on Oriental studies in London in 1874. Religious and social reformers like Raja Ram Mohan Roy (1772–1833), Ishwar Chandra Vidyasagar (1820–91), and the writer and teacher Dayanand Saraswati (1824–83), all contributed, through their writings and speeches, to the spirit of nationalism and the independence movement. Swami Vivekananda (1863–1902) introduced the philosophy of Vedanta and yoga to the western world, also having a tremendous influence on the people of India, especially through his political agitation. Books by the British in any of the Indian languages are almost unheard of, apart from the translations by the early Orientalists.

Rajendralal Mitra.

Swami Vivekananda.

Toru Dutt

The most outstanding 19th-century Indian woman of literature, a natural linguist fluent in English and French, was Toru Dutt (1856–77), who studied at Cambridge between 1871 and 1873, translated French poems into English, and was the first Indian to write novels in French and to make a mark in literature at such a young age.

The national conscience aroused by the main Indian press and literature in vernacular as well as English found its most glorious recognition when in 1913 the poet Rabindranath Tagore (1861–1941), author of *Gitanjali*, became the first non-European winner of the Nobel Prize for Literature.

Pre-eminent among British writers chronicling the days of the Raj was Rudyard Kipling (1865–1936), who was born in India and earned fame and fortune for works including his *Jungle Books*, *Kim*, *Plain Tales from the Hills* and his poems about Gunga Din. George Orwell called Kipling the 'prophet of British Imperialism', and his contribution to the fund for General Dyer, responsible for the 1919 Amritsar massacre, is seen as an act of betrayal by many. Countless British authors have taken the British Raj as their subject, the most distinguished of them including E M Forster (1879–1970), with his classic novel *A Passage to India*, Paul Scott (1920–78), author of the Raj Quartet novels subsequently dramatized for television as *The Jewel in the Crown*, J G Farrell (1935–79), with *The Siege of Krishnapur*, part of his *Empire Trilogy*, based on the Indian Mutiny, and M M Kaye, who was born in India and wrote *The Far Pavilions*, an epic romance that gained worldwide success. The television and film adaptations of these works brought them all international recognition.

After Indian Independence in 1947, the mood changed for the new generation of writers, Indian and British. They moved away from writing about nationalism and reforms and instead wrote fiction, especially historical novels, which were well received in both countries. A number received the prestigious Booker Prize for the best novel in English published by a British or Commonwealth author, some more than once, becoming internationally well-known and celebrities at various literary festivals.

Top of the list is Salman Rushdie, knighted in 2007 for services to literature, who is best remembered for his novel *Midnight's Children*, which won not only the Booker Prize in 1981, but also the 'Booker of Bookers' in 2008, for the best book ever to have won the award.

Anita Desai was shortlisted three times for the Booker Prize and won the British *Guardian* award for her novel *The Village by the Sea* in 1983.

Arundhati Roy, equally distinguished as a political activist, won the Booker Prize in 1997 for *The God of Small Things*, and Kiran Desai won it in 2006 for her novel *The Inheritance of Loss*. In 2008 Aravind Adiga won it for his debut novel *The White Tiger*. To this list must be added the names of Booker nominated authors, Vikram Seth, best known for his huge novel *A Suitable Boy*, and Amitav Ghosh for *Sea of Poppies*.

The most successful East–West partnership in the entertainment business was that between the novelist and screenwriter Ruth Prawer Jhabvala (1927–2013) and the film producers and directors Ismail Merchant (1936–2005) and James Ivory. Jhabvala's novel *Heat and Dust* won her the Booker Prize and subsequently became a Merchant-Ivory film, for which she wrote the screenplay. Among their many collaborations were two films of E M Forster's novels, *Howards End* and *A Room With A View*. Which won two Academy Awards and one BAFTA.

Today there is a new vitality in literature and the entertainment business that crosses all boundaries of cultural, religious and language difference, and exerts a powerful influence on the artists of the East as much as the West, be they Indian or British.

Rudyard Kipling.

E M Forster.

Salman Rushdie.

Arundhati Roy.

Vikramjit Kakati

Cartoons

Political cartoons first appeared in India in 1850 in the English-owned *Bengal Hurkaru* and the *Indian Gazette*. In Britain magazines like *Punch* (1841–1992), *Fun* (1861–1901), and the *Pall Mall Gazette* (1865–1921) had created a popular interest in these illustrative comments on current events. In 1872 *Anand Bazar Patrika* became the first Indian-owned newspaper to carry political cartoons.

During the period of India's struggle for freedom from the autocratic rule of the British, there was no shortage of cartoonists who ridiculed the popular figures of the day, addressing both the British rule in India and Indian society, but especially the inequalities of the Raj.

Cartoons have no language barriers, so even illiterate people can understand them, to the extent that some politicians fear them more than written attacks. Often accompanied by a caption, cartoons make use of the elements of caricature; with unsuppressed sarcasm, humour and wit, they make fierce pictorial comment on contemporary issues.

Right: Two engravings from *Tom Raw*, a poem describing the adventures of a cadet in the East India company's service, illustrated by Sir Charles D'Oyly.

"MENDING THE LESSON."

POLITICAL ECONOMY. "TAKE CARE, MY DEAR JOHN. DON'T INTERFERE WITH THE LAWS OF SUPPLY AND DEMAND."
JOHN BULL. "I DON'T, MISS PRUDENCE. SHE *DEMANDS* AND I *SUPPLY*."

Hindi Punch, 1873.

Left: Protest cartoon against the famine of 1942.

Left: cartoon depicting Dadabhai Naoroji, the first Indian MP at Westminster, as Othello, *Hindi Punch*.

A selection of political cartoons from *Hindi Punch*.

VICTORIA REGINA ET IMPERATRIX.
Shade of Lord Beaconsfield. "Now—you remember Me!"

THE NEW YEAR'S GIFT.

Pam (to Sir Colin). "Well—upon my word—eh!—I'm really extremely obliged to you—but—eh!—how about keeping the brute?"

Fashion and Textiles from India

Anne-Marie Benson

Textile and Fan Specialist and Consultant, Former Head of the
Textile Department of Phillips International Auctioneers and
Former President of Fan Circle International

How lucky the English were as the beautiful cottons in fine muslin or quality calico arrived on the shores from India in the 17th Century. They were exotic, expensive and desirable.

Founded in London in 1600, The Honourable East India Company was established on the west coast of India in 1615 and by 1632 there were trading centres in Madras, Calcutta and Bombay. Famous for their fine muslins, the Bengalis sent piece goods, or yardage, to England via agents of the Company throughout the 18th Century and into the early 19th Century. Dacca was especially known for white work, a white embroidered muslin called Chikan. In the 18th Century the English ladies used this for sleeve ruffles, cape collars with pendant ends, called pelerines, kerchiefs and aprons and in the early 1800s for dresses and summer shawls.

Berhampur on the River Hooghly in Bengal exported tie-dyed silk piece goods, some of which displayed patterns of handkerchiefs or scarves to be cut and finished in England. Such items of costume became popular with the working classes. More detailed tie-dyed and printed silks came from Gujarat in the west.

In the South of India along the Coromandel Coast, which stretched from the mouths of the River Krishna down to the Palk Strait, the Indians produced a marvellous chintz. Using cotton cloth chintz is made by a complex method of preparation, dyeing, painting and printing. It is thought to be one of India's best textiles and it arrived in quantity from the late 17th Century and throughout most of the 18th Century from the Madras trading centre. With a myriad of colours and designs primarily of animals, flowers and leaves, this fabric was used variously. It was used for bed hangings, coverlets and furnishings, as well as gentlemens' undress caps and banyans, a type of loose skirted indoor coat, and for womens' dresses and jackets. Towards the end of the 18th Century tastes and styles changed and delicate or rather dainty patterns became popular. New designs were adapted to suit the fashion, but in essence chintz was no longer the material of choice. Chintz was also produced in the north west of India, in Gujarat.

In England shawls became very fashionable in the latter part of the 18th Century, probably for a number of reasons. For the woman, surely, the successful pairing of the Kashmir shawl with the sparsely patterned, light weight muslin or plain silk dresses so fashionable at the time must be one reason. Another quite simply warmth. Woven in goat's hair, and called pashmina, the Kashmir shawl had a plain centre with a row of upright flowering stems or cones to each end, which were worked in coloured threads. Kashmir shawls remained popular throughout the 19th Century, but changed in design and size to follow the fashions.

As happened in many areas, the Industrial Revolution changed the textile trade in India dramatically: it went into a noticeable decline. During the 18th Century there had been import restrictions to manage and these were creatively overcome. But with Britain using the machine swiftly and producing new designs in quantity from the second half of the 19th Century, it was not possible for the Indians to compete. There were of course exceptions. The shop, Liberty & Co. of London, displayed a selection of stock in their India Pavilion at the Paris Universal Exhibition of 1889 and this included a variety of shawls, muslins, embroideries and tussore silks from Delhi, Dacca, Amritsar and Kashmir.

It was not until the 1960s that Indian textiles and fashion returned as an influence in Britain. However, the style was more Indian than British. During the Summers women wore ankle length dresses showing a sari influence. Both men and women used, wore and were influenced by the colourful embroidery of the Punjab and Rajasthan, the intricate needlework of Surat, the printed work of Madras and the South of India, the tie-dyes of Gujarat and tambour work of Bengal.

The popular paisley design on a shawl and a sari.

In conclusion, whilst looking at the fashions of today, both in costume and furnishing fabrics, it is quite safe to say the Indian influence in Britain has not disappeared.

CHAPTER 16

The Indian Contribution to the Two World Wars

There were two Indian armies in India: one before the Mutiny of 1857 under the control of the East India Company and the second, under the British Crown; following the Government of India Act of 1858, which called for the liquidation of the East India Company and had its activities transferred to the Crown.

When the East India Company first established itself in India, its security was maintained by a few watchmen protecting its trading centres and factories. However, with the success of their mercantile activities, it soon became necessary to have an improved defence force. It was able to take charge of the garrison at Bombay resulting in the formation of a military unit the forerunner of the Indian Army.

The Company maintained a strong presence in Bengal, Bombay, and Madras, their three Presidencies. Over the next hundred years, its activities spread across the country, until the Mutiny brought a sudden end to its military authority.

The British Indian Army included Hindus, Sikhs, Muslims and Christians and growing over the years and remaining the principal army of India until independence in 1947. It became a very significant part of the British forces in the two world wars. The armies were identified by their names, the Indian Army was the force recruited in India. The British Army in India consisted of British Army Units, posted to India and the Army of India included both the Indian Army and the British Army in India.

Below left: Indian soldiers served in all theatres of WWI from the freezing trenches of the Western Front to the heat of Abyssinia.

Below: Many Indian WWI casualties were cared for at the makeshift hospital set up in the Royal Pavilion, Brighton.

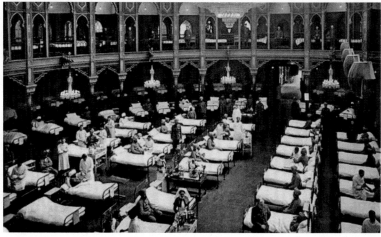

Above: Paving stone in the National Memorial Arboretum commemorating Khudadad Khan the first Indian to be awarded the Victoria Cross in 1914.

Right: Portrait of Khudadad Khan.

The history of the Indian Army is the history of a remarkable group of Indian men. Armed with courage and loyalty, they safeguarded the property of the East India Company in India and died, defending Britain in the two world wars, on the battlefields of Europe.

The First World War

At the outbreak of both the World Wars, India's enemy was Britain, not Germany. Yet at a time when Indian national leaders were campaigning to end British rule and being imprisoned, millions of ordinary Indians enlisted to fight against the German offensive. The Indian war effort was truly immense. Huge sums of money were given outright to Britain, as well as military requirements such as summer uniforms, boots, sandbags, parachutes and munitions and humanitarian essentials such as ambulances, hospital ships and medical supplies.

All opposition to the British government ceased at the beginning of the First World War, and the feelings of Indians at large were well summed up by Pandit Madan Mohan Malaviya, an ex-President of the Indian National Congress. When the war was only five weeks old, he assured the Viceroy that India would grudge 'no sacrifice of men and money in order that the British armies shall triumph.' India gave £100 million immediately to Britain, followed by an annual contribution of between £20 and £30 million towards war expenses.

But it was in the field of manpower that India made her greatest contribution. By the end of the war India had sent over a million men overseas. Impressive as they are, the numbers that really linger in the mind are the casualty rolls: over 74,000 dead and over 64,000 wounded. The Indians fought like tigers: even their German enemies were to say that they were 'not to be underrated.' These Indian soldiers had pride in themselves and in their honour. King George V, recognising the courage with which they fought in France, sent a personal message to them:

'You are the descendants of men who have been great rulers and great warriors... You will recall the glories of your race... Hindus and Muslims will be fighting side by side with British soldiers and our gallant French allies... You will be the first Indian soldiers who will have the honour of showing Europe that the sons of India have lost none of their ancient martial instincts... In battle you will remember that your religions enjoin on you that to give your life doing your duty is your highest reward... From mosques and temples prayers are ascending to the God of all. You will fight for your King and your faith, so that history will record the doings of India's sons and your children will proudly tell of the deeds of their fathers...'

Below left: Peace Memorial Garden, Horsell Commons, dedicated to the Muslim soldiers of British Indian Army WWI.

Below: Graves of the WWI Muslim soldiers, in Brookwood Cemetery, the largest in Britain.

As Britain and the world commemorate the centenary of the Great War it is a worthy reminder of the Indian contribution and their supreme sacrifice.

For their gallantry and valour, eleven Indian soldiers were awarded the Victoria Cross. Before 1911 Indians were not eligible for this award.

Khudadad Khan (1888–1971) was the first Indian to be awarded the Victoria Cross only a few weeks after the start of the First World War. He was fighting with the British forces on the Western Front in October 1914 in the Duke of Connaught's Own Baluchis Indian Army. His machine-gun team kept their guns in action preventing the Germans making the final assault until their gun was disabled by a shell killing everyone except Khan. Although himself wounded, Khan managed to crawl back to his regiment. Thanks to his bravery, the Germans were held up long enough for Indian and British reinforcements to arrive, stopping the Germans from reaching vital points. For his wounds, Khan was treated in the hospital in Brighton. Three months later he received his VC from King George V at Buckingham Palace. The citation reads:

> On 31 October, at Hollenbeck, Belgium, the British officer in charge of the detachment having been wounded, and the other gun put out of action by a shell, Sepoy (soldier) Khudadad, though himself wounded, remained working his gun until all other five men of the gun detachment had been killed.

Khan returned to India and continued to serve in the Indian Army. He spent the last years of his life in Pakistan and the VC he was awarded is proudly on show in the village where he was born, Dab in Chakwal District, Punjab. Other machine gunners of Khan's party were given posthumous awards of the Indian Order of Merit and the Distinguished Service Medal.

As the war wore on, the perpetual danger out in the battlefield, high casualty figures, the sustained loss of men to wounds, the bitter cold and wet weather, became too much for some Indian soldiers, causing them to suffer from exhaustion and depression. The incidence of self-inflicted wounds grew, and the mood became one of fatalistic despair. The main topics of letters home were hopelessness and misery. However, after a period of rest and restored strength, these men fought well and gained admiration and honour for their achievements.

After the war India wanted a rapid advance towards the free Dominion status enjoyed by Canada and Australia, and it was very much hoped that Britain would, by way of appreciation of its immense contribution of men and money to the war effort, make the much-demanded constitutional changes. Instead, the government became more hostile, banning all political activities and imprisoning members of the Home Rule League established by Bal Gangadhar Tilak and Annie Besant. Indian troops returned home with their faith in British leadership broken.

Between the wars

The period between the two wars was a time of constant agitation and disorder in India. In 1919, only five months after the end of the First World War, there was the horror of the Amritsar Massacre. In 1928 Lala Lajpat Rai was beaten by the police during a peaceful protest against the Simon Commission and later died from his wounds. The Dandi Salt March in 1930 in opposition to British Salt Tax, sparked a nationwide campaign of civil disobedience. Bhagat Singh was convicted and executed in 1931, after he shot a British police officer in revenge for the killing of Lala Lajpat Rai, and the two Round Table Conferences in London in 1930 and 1931. In 1939, before the start of the Second World War, nearly 100,000 Indians were imprisoned for their anti-British activities. The British government had a deliberate policy of treating political prisoners worse than convicts, and they were dealt with severely, including public floggings.

The Second World War

On 3 September 1939 when the Second World War began, the Viceroy of India, the Marquess of Linlithgow, declared war against Germany without taking into his confidence any of the Indian leaders. It was only after sending Indian troops to various theatres of war that he consulted them. The Working Committee of the Congress met and, after prolonged deliberation, passed a resolution declaring that 'if Great Britain was fighting for the maintenance and extension of democracy, then she must necessarily end imperialism in her own possession and establish full democracy in India'.

On 27 July 1940, another resolution was passed by the Congress in which an

King George VI inspecting Indian troops during the early years of the War.

offer of co-operation in the war was made, provided that India's demand for independence was accepted and a provisional National Government responsible to the
then Central Assembly was formed. The response from Britain, that it 'could not
contemplate transfer of their present responsibilities', disappointed the Congress.

But its disapproval made no difference to recruitment. The result was a remarkable body of men, the largest volunteer army in history. Hindu, Sikh and Muslim soldiers joined forces and served shoulder to shoulder with their British counterparts.
Over two and a half million Indians came to the colours without conscription.

However, thousands of pro-Congress men and women were jailed and many
were killed when police fired on anti-British crowds during the war. A small but
significant number of Indian troops joined Subhash Chandra Bose's Indian National
Army which fought with the Japanese against the British.

The Indian women who volunteered their services to the war efforts are largely
overlooked. The Women's Auxiliary Corps India (WACI), was formed in 1942 for non-
combatant roles. Women volunteers worked behind the front lines as drivers,
administrators and switchboard operators, wherever the army went. They wore
military uniforms with different styles of hats and was the only women's military
service in India that provided personnel to serve with the airforce and the navy, the
latter renamed the WRINS. The 11,000-strong Corps was eventually disbanded when
India became independent in 1947.

The WRINS, Women's Royal Indian Naval Service, fulfilled many essential roles
releasing men to join the armed forces, and contributing significantly to the running
of the Royal Navy shore establishments. Wearing a uniform of white sari with a blue
border, and working in the Army offices, their jobs included cypher coding, wireless
communications, typing, logging, filing and checking messages. Sadly, the memorial to

Below: Field Marshal Auchinleck
inspecting members of the
Women's Auxiliary Corps (India).

Right: WRINS in India wearing
their traditional sari uniforms.

the women of the Second World War in Whitehall, unveiled by the Queen in 2005, does not include either the WACI or the WRINS.

Another woman who offered her services to the war efforts was Princess Indira of Kapurthala, who drove ambulances in London, recovering casualties of the Blitz and taking them to hospital. She also presented a BBC radio programme three times a week for the benefit of the Indian forces in the Middle East, giving them information about the war, and famously came to be known as the 'Radio Princess'. For a time she also turned her hand to the responsible job of postal censorship.

An unusual and significant help for the Indian soldiers came from another remarkable woman, Cornelia Sorabji. She conceived the idea of publishing a very special kind of book *Queen Mary's Book for India*, a compilation of tributes to the Indian soldiers from prominent, mainly British public figures. Her request to the Prime Minister, Winston Churchill, was answered by his wife, Clementine with the comment that, as her husband was rather busy with the war, Cornelia was at liberty to quote from his broadcasts or speeches, she chose his speech of 14 July 1940:

'All now depends upon the whole life-strength of the British race in every part of the world and of all our associated peoples and of all well-wishers in every land doing their utmost night and day, giving all, daring all, enduring all – to the utmost, to the end.'

Above left: Queen Mary.

Above centre: Lt Preminder Singh Bhagat the first Indian to receive the VC during World War II.

Above: Princess Indira of Kapurthala.

Amongst the contributors, were Field-Marshall Sir Archibald Wavell, the Rt Hon Ernest Bevin, the Marchioness of Linlithgow, T S Eliot, Dorothy L Sayers and Lt Preminder Singh Bhagat, the first Indian to be awarded the Victoria Cross in the Second World War.

Queen Mary herself wrote a message for the book, paying tribute to the courage and the sacrifices of the Indian soldiers, and understanding the anxieties of their families at home:

'I send this message to the mothers of India's fighting men:

You are constantly in my thoughts and I know that many of you are anxious, and some are sorrowful, but all are proud of your brave sons.

My own dear sons have served in the Navy, Army and Air Force and I share your anxieties, your sorrows and your pride. I do not forget the patient fortitude of your daughters-in-law and I trust that your gentle care sustains them in this time of trial.

I pray that God may bless all gallant Indian soldiers, sailors, and airmen and that in the hour of victory they may return with great honour to their homes and make your hearts glad again.'

In his Foreword, the Secretary of State for India, the Rt Hon L S Amery, wrote,

'Never in her history, not even in the last war, has India made an effort comparable either in volume or in quality with that which she is making to-day. She has contributed to the sea war a Navy ever growing in number and efficiency, as well as the indispensable service of some forty thousand merchant seamen...'

The book was published in 1943, with the proceeds going to the Indian Comforts Fund to care for Indian prisoners of war in Germany.

Preminder Singh Bhagat (1918–75) was the first Indian to be awarded the Victoria Cross in the Second World War. A Second Lieutenant in the Royal Bombay Sappers and Mines, in 1940 Bhagat was in command of a field company in Abyssinia on mobile troop trucks clearing up Italian mines on the roads. On two occasions his carrier was blown up but he refused relief. He travelled over 55 miles through enemy territory before being ambushed. His success brought him promotion to the rank of Lt General in the Corps of the Indian Engineers, and he was awarded the Victoria Cross for bravery. The citation reads,

'His coolness for a period of 98 hours, and his persistence and gallantry not only in battle but throughout the long period during which the safety of the column and the speed at which it could advance, were dependent on his personal efforts, which were of the highest order. 31st January 1941.'

Lt Preminder Singh Bhagat's contribution to *Queen Mary's Book for India.*

I have the honour of serving in the Royal Bombay Sappers and Miners. This group is composed of Indians recruited from the Punjab and the Deccan. This it is composed of people who come from about one-third of India. They are Mohammedans and Sikhs from Punjab and Hindus (Mahrattas) from Deccan.

Not only have the Sappers stuck to making tracks and repairing demolitions, but they have had to lead the advance, clearing mine-fields and obstacles. In one advance into Abyssinia one party of Sappers worked three days without rest, cleaning mine-fields. They were doing this under air attacks and surprise enemy ground attacks. In spite of this, after three days, they were as keen as ever to go on.

Many a daring story can be written about the Indian Sapper, but it is best that the noble record should come out after the conclusion of this war.

Between 1939 and 1945, over two million Indians served alongside other Allied forces. They fought in all theatres during WWII and a total of 30 Victoria Crosses were awarded to Indian soldiers for their outstanding bravery.

Bhagat returned to India to a hero's welcome; the Victoria Cross was presented to him at a formal investiture ceremony held at Viceroy Linlithgow's Palace in Delhi, the first time a VC was ever awarded by a Viceroy. At the General Bhagat Museum in India his medals, photographs, press cuttings and uniform are displayed, to encourage future generations to join the Bombay Sappers. His Victoria Cross is on display in the Bombay Sappers Centre.

Throughout the war a relationship of mutual trust and respect existed between the British and Indian officers. Their bravery and skilled efficiency earned them admiration and awards. For their courage, 30 Indian soldiers were decorated with the Victoria Cross.

The Indian Army, the Indian SOE, the WRINS and the WACI played very important roles in the two World Wars. Their timely support constituted the largest volunteer army in the history of modern warfare. By the end of the war, the Indian Army had become a professional and accomplished force equipped to deal successfully with the problems and complications of modern warfare.

A Life of Bravery

By Shrabani Basu

Chair, Noor Inayat Khan Memorial Trust, and author of *Spy Princess*

Noor Inayat Khan (1914–44), a descendant of the legendary Tipu Sultan, was a British agent who was dropped behind enemy lines in the Second World War in Europe. Born in Moscow to an Indian father, Hazrat Inayat Khan, and American mother, Ora Ray Baker, Noor was the first woman radio operator to be infiltrated into occupied France. She was also a talented writer of children's stories, and was celebrating the publication of her first book, *Twenty Jataka Tales*, when war broke out in Europe in 1939.

In London, Noor signed up for the Women's Auxiliary Air Force (WAAF) and began training as a radio operator. Her knowledge of and familiarity with Paris were noted by the Special Operations Executive (SOE), a crack group set up by Churchill to 'set Europe ablaze', and Noor was recruited and trained to become a secret agent. On a full-moon night in the summer of 1943, she was flown to France. Armed only with a false passport, a pistol and some French francs, she started her dangerous mission.

Paris during the war was the most difficult place for an agent to operate in, as it was crawling with members of the Gestapo. Within a week of her landing, disaster struck her circuit, and her colleagues were arrested. London asked Noor to return, but she refused, as she was the last radio link left between London and Paris. Noor worked alone in Paris, rebuilding the circuit single-handedly, doing the work of six radio operators. She played a cat-and-mouse game with the Gestapo, dyeing her hair, changing her place of transmission, and outwitting them at every step. They laid several traps for her but could not catch her.

However, Noor's luck ran out. She was betrayed and arrested. She made two daring escapes but was re-arrested. By now labelled 'highly dangerous', she was transported to the Pforzheim prison in Germany, where she was shackled and kept in isolation, half-starved and beaten regularly. Despite repeated interrogation and torture, Noor revealed nothing about her colleagues and gave away no secrets. Ten months later she was transported with three other colleagues to Dachau Concentration Camp, where she was tortured and shot. Her last word was 'Liberté'.

Noor was awarded the highest civilian honours by Britain and France, the George Cross and the Croix de Guerre with Gold Star. She is remembered in France as 'Madeleine of the Resistance'. Madeleine was Noor's code name.

The bust of Noor Inayat Khan unveiled by HRH Princess Anne in Gordon Square, Euston, London 2012. In 2014, the Royal Mail issued a stamp honouring Noor. In 2018 a campaign was started to feature her on the redesigned £50 note. She is to be honoured with a blue plaque, the first for an Indian woman, at 4 Taviton Street, where she lived during the war.

CHAPTER 17

Indian National Congress

British imperialism is often held to have been at its most uncivil on occupied Indian territory, and yet the organisation that brought India's much desired freedom, the Indian National Congress, resulted from the efforts of a Briton, Allan Octavian Hume. He was the man who in 1885 successfully won the support of like-minded, mostly western-educated Indians for the formation of a political party for mass agitation against the British in India.

Hume, who became a long-serving Secretary of the Indian National Congress, was one of many British friends of India, among them Keir Hardie, Florence Nightingale, Annie Besant, Ramsay Macdonald, H N Brailsford and others.

The first session of the Indian National Congress took place in Bombay in 1885 with 72 delegates, presided over by W C Bonnerjee. Three years later, in 1888, George Yule became the first of six British presidents, followed by Sir William Wedderburn in 1889 and 1919, Alfred Webb in 1894, Henry Cotton in 1904, Annie Besant in 1917 – when she also hoisted the third (in design) Indian flag during the First World War and the Home Rule Movement – and Mrs Nellie Sen Gupta in 1934.

Though other minor political parties existed at local levels, it was the Indian

Right: Keir Hardie.

Far right: W C Bonnerjee.

National Congress that developed into a nationwide movement and became the voice of India. It was the enemy of imperial British Government, but never of the British people. To inform friends of India in Britain about the party's activities, aims and objectives, in 1889 the Congress established a British Committee of the Indian National Congress in London, its objective was to create an awareness of social conditions in India and of how India was governed by British bureaucrats. In 1890 the Committee also launched *India*, a journal, which was at times financially supported by Sir William Wedderburn and A O Hume. There have been unsuccessful efforts in India to establish a memorial to Hume, who 'liked to be remembered with affection, if not gratitude' by its people.

Towards Independence

If and when Britain left India, it was to do so on condition that India satisfy five prerequisites:

1   Indianisation of the civil service should occur to such a degree that the function of government could be carried on.

2   Agreement between Hindus and Muslims as to the respective powers of the two communities, with guarantees to other minorities.

3   Signs that law and order could be maintained.

4   The obligations and treaties the British Government had given to the separate Native States should be respected.

5   India should be kept within the Empire.

This was during the Second World War, when Britain had not yet decided to leave India, and at this point agreement on or realisation of all, or even any, of these conditions was considered impossible.

The Second World War, however, made an immense impact on Britain, leaving it utterly impoverished – indeed, little short of bankrupt. On 12 August 1946, therefore, Lord Wavell, the Viceroy, wrote in his diary that he had told leaders of loyalist landholders that:

> '... it is better to be honest and say that we are going to hand over power; that it is right to do so and leave Indians to govern themselves, that while the Congress is not a body one would have chosen as representatives of the great mass of the Indian people, it is the body the Indian people have chosen themselves and we have to deal with the men of their choice.'

British Prime Minister Ramsay MacDonald to the right of Gandhi at the Second Round Table Conference in London, October 1931.

Within ten years of the India Act of 1935, the British position had changed. But by now Indians were not prepared to accept anything less than total independence. And though Wavell talked about the Congress, many Muslims were fearful of being disadvantaged in a Congress-ruled India, and there now emerged the new and powerful Muslim League, led by Mohammed Ali Jinnah. With the League's success in the general election of 1946, the Congress's vision of a strong and united India, and the British Labour government's decision to give up power as soon as possible, the partition of India became inevitable. The bloodshed that followed, with the deaths of over 200,000 men, women and children, was a high price to pay for freedom.

India did not pursue or seek retribution for 200 years of British rule. Calls for Britain to pay reparations over the Raj were irrelevant and impractical.

CHAPTER 18
Freedom Fighters Remembered

In the struggle for independence, there were many, both Indian and British who united against British rule in India. Their names have faded and their heroic deeds been reduced to fragments of history. They never get mentioned at Independence and Republic Day celebrations, the very cause for which they made great sacrifices. There is never a roll-call of their names, either in speeches or in the published programmes of such events. But the lives of all India's freedom fighters, not just the usual one or two, need to be studied and analysed, and their determined campaigns for self-government recognised. Understanding the past, and the part they played in it, helps us recognise where we come from. It also gives us an opportunity to do better. As the British MP Edward Gibson (1737–94) rightly said, 'I know no way of judging the future but by the past.'

Womesh Chandra Bonnerjee (1844–1906) studied law at Middle Temple and was the fourth Indian to be called to the Bar in England, in 1867. A founder member of the Indian National Congress, and its first President in 1885, he believed that the Congress should limit its activities to political matters only, leaving the question of social reforms to other organisations. A successful lawyer, he lived in England and had chambers in Lincoln's Inn, and continued to promote the cause of India until his death. With Dadabhai Naoroji he started the London India Society.

Lokmanya Gangadhar Tilak.

Lokmanya Gangadhar Tilak (1856–1920) was a staunch Hindu who wanted Hindi to become the national language of India. Regarded as the father of Indian unrest, he was the man most determined to expel the British from India. Though he was once influenced by English idealists, he came to reject many features of western ideology and society. India should demand constitutional changes from its British rulers, he maintained, rather than beg for it.

In 1895 he started the Shivaji Movement to encourage India's youth to remove foreigners from India. In 1897 he was arrested and later sent to prison in Burma for six years. At the start of the First World War, he encouraged Indians to help the British government, expecting the British to do the same for Indians. Halfway through the war he changed his mind and asked the Indians to withdraw support, mocking the British, 'that they were willing to share everything with Indians except power'. He asked the Indian National Congress to change its policy and defy the government, even if it meant using violence. Because of his frequent imprisonment he was unable to take an active part in the struggle for independence.

Shyamaji Krishnavarma.

Indian Journals, published from London during the Raj, some as voices of the Indian National Congress: *The Asiatic* (1869); *The Statesman* (1869); *India* (1890); *The Indian Socialist* (1905); *The Bande Mataram* (1909); *The Indiaman* (1914); *United India* (1920); *Hind* (1921); *The India News* (1929) and *India Bulletin* (1932). *India* was launched in London by Dadabhai Naoroji and Sir William Wedderburn in February 1890.

Shyamaji Krishnavarma (1857–1930) was one of the foremost freedom fighters in India's struggle for independence. Yet today he is barely acknowledged or admired for the risks he took, the sacrifices he made or his selfless service to the nation.

Born in Mandavi, Gujarat, Krishnavarma came to England in 1879 to study at Balliol College, Oxford. He became member of the Royal Society of the Inner Temple and was called to the Bar in 1884. On his return to India in 1885, he served the Maharana of Udaipur as a Council Member for two years. A bitter experience in 1897 with a British agent shook his faith in the British rule in India, with the result that his only mission in life became the training of young men and women to fight for the liberty of the motherland. In particular, it was the barbarous punishment, even imprisonment, of freedom fighters that made him come to London in 1902 to fight for India's freedom.

Krishnavarma bought a house, the India House, in Highgate, north London. It was often visited by Tilak, Gokhale, Lala Lajpat Rai, Gandhi, Lenin and many others sympathetic to his views and activities for the justice for India. In 1905 he embarked on a new career, launching the monthly journal *The Indian Sociologist*, the voice of India in Britain for freedom, justice and reforms. He also founded the Indian Home Rule Society, giving him and his supporters an additional platform for anti-British propaganda, with the aim of inspiring mass opposition to British rule in India. His inflammatory statements in print and speeches were closely monitored by the British authorities, and in 1909 the Inner Temple disbarred him for his anti-British activities.

Before the British Government could capture and detain him, Krishnavarma secretly left London in 1907 and moved his headquarters to Paris for some years, finally moving to Geneva just before the start of the First World War in 1914. The publication of *The Indian Sociologist* was suspended during the war; Krishnavarma began editing the journal again in 1920 and continued until his death in Geneva in 1930.

The British authorities suppressed the news of Krishnavarma's death in India, and his ashes remained in Geneva until they were repatriated to his home town in 2003, 56 years after Indian independence. In November 2015, the Honourable Society of the Inner Temple decided to reinstate Shyamaji Krishnavarma as a member once again.

Sadly many, like Krishnavarma, who dedicated their lives fighting for India's freedom, are eclipsed by the activities of those who came later in the run-up to independence. It has been a struggle to reinstate their names in the roll of honour at celebrations marking Indian independence and Republic Day anniversaries.

Bhikaji Cama.

Bhikaji Cama (1861–1936), the 'Mother of all Indian Revolutions', holds a unique and special position in the history of India's struggle for freedom. She demanded complete and immediate independence, to see the Raj reduced to 'dust and ashes'. To her, the British, practising the worst form of imperialism, were keeping the country in abject poverty by helping themselves to India's wealth, over £35 million annually.

In 1902, for personal and health reasons, Bhikaji Cama came to London, the country of her 'enemy', determined to promote India's right to independence. British intelligence watched her activities, and her campaigns featured in many reports, and it hatched a plot to 'finish her off'. Suspecting their intentions, Cama escaped to France.

During her time in London Madam Cama was personal secretary to Dadabhai Naoroji, which gave her the opportunity of meeting other Europeans sympathetic to India's cause. She rapidly became the most well-known Indian woman in Europe, and was invited as a delegate to the International Socialist Congress at Stuttgart in 1907. There she delivered an impressive speech about the 'terrible tyrannies' under British rule in India, and made history by unfurling the Indian national flag for the first time ever outside India. 'This flag of Indian Independence!' she declared: 'Behold, it is born! It has been made sacred by the blood of young Indians who sacrificed their lives. I call upon you gentlemen to rise and salute this flag of Independence'.

On 10 September 1909, Madam Cama brought out at her own expense, from a base in Geneva, the revolutionary monthly journal *The Bande Mataram*. There was no doubt about her motivation, as her first editorial made quite clear:

We owe no apology to the world in general and to the Indian people in particular for appearing before them. In fact we regret that we did not begin our work earlier in the year. Ever since the suppression of the famous journal, the *Bande Mataram*, in India, the need of a similar paper, conducted on advanced lines, has been felt among all circles of Indian Nationalists. The tyranny of the British government has rendered it impossible to preach our principles through the Press from within our own country.

Described as 'a monthly organ of Indian Independence', the journal, published until 1913, was smuggled into India.

During her years in Europe Madam Cama was really an unofficial ambassador, pleading India's cause. Among the many people she met was Lenin, who sympa-

Right: Pandit Madan Mohan Malaviya.

Far right: Lala Lajpat Rai.

thised with her and admired her determination to fight for India. Even those who disagreed with her could not fail to recognise the dignity and dedication with which this lone Indian woman put her argument that the British rule in India had to cease.

After 33 years as a political activist, often at great personal risk, Bhikaji Cama was eventually allowed to return to India in 1936, because of her failing health. Sadly, she died shortly afterwards, 11 years before seeing the Indian tricolour officially hoisted in independent India's capital, New Delhi, on 15 August 1947.

Pandit Madan Mohan Malaviya (1861–1946) was a Sanskrit scholar and three times President of the Indian National Congress. He came to England with Gandhi in 1931 for the Second Round Table Conference and was active in the non-co-operation movement, rejecting the politics of appeasement. A moderate politician, Malaviya was against a separate electorate for the Muslims. He left the Congress and started the Congress National Party. Always wearing white earned him the nickname 'the spotless Pandit'.

Lala Lajpat Rai (1865–1928), a lawyer and politician, joined the Indian National Congress and came to England on its behalf to win over British public opinion in favour of responsible government for Indians. His patriotism and political activities were such that the government exiled him to Burma for six months, a punishment that made him even more determined to fight for India's freedom. In 1914 he visited England as a member of the Congress delegation, and then spent eight years in America to escape political harassment for his political views and activities. In 1928 he led a peaceful anti-Simon Commission procession in Lahore, where he was the target of a brutal *lathi* (baton) charge. At a meeting the same evening, Rai remarked with vigour that 'Every blow aimed at me is a nail in the coffin of British imperialism.' Three days later he succumbed to his fatal injuries.

Gopal Krishna Gokhale (1866–1915) was known as the greatest leader of the Indian National Congress, becoming its President in 1905. Gokhale believed in the maintenance of law and order, and was an idealist who believed in inter-racial goodwill. It was his belief that self-government 'had to be earned by Indian assimilation of the British Way.' A voice of moderation and spokesman for Indian opinion in Bombay and the Imperial Legislative Council, he found himself dubbed 'fainthearted' by the extremists and a 'seditionist in disguise' by the reactionaries.

Mohandas Karamchand Gandhi (1869–1948), freedom fighter and social reformer, studied law at Inner Temple in 1887 and returned to India in 1891. He was the President of the Indian National Congress in 1924 and led the 'Salt March' to the Dandi coast in 1930 in defiance of government's tax on salt. In 1931 Gandhi came to London for the Second Round Table Conference. He set up the India Conciliation Group and chose civil disobedience, non-co-operation and fasting as weapons to fight British injustice. Like other nationalist freedom fighters, he was frequently in and out of jail, ironically serving time for his 'Quit India' movement in 1942 during the Second World War at a time when Indian soldiers were dying for Britain's fight for freedom. Gandhi failed to persuade M A Jinnah against partition.

Gopal Krishna Gokhale.

Mohandas Karamchand Gandhi.

Sardar Vallabhbhai Patel.

Rt Hon Sri V S Srinivasa Sastri.

Rt Hon Sri V S Srinivasa Sastri (1869–1946) was an academic, scholar and politician whose knowledge of English earned him a reputation as the 'silver-tongued orator of the British Empire'. He preferred India to remain in the Commonwealth and secure independence by constitutional means. In 1931 he attended the Imperial Conference in London, which was a great success, and after winning many British hearts was made a Privy Councillor. In 1931 he attended the Second Round Table Conference in London, and went on to plead for self-rule for India at many more international conferences, winning laurels through his impressive personality, statesmanship and matchless powers of oratory. Sastri was twice offered a knighthood by the British, but refused.

Sardar Vallabhbhai Patel (1875–1950), barrister, statesman and the best prime minister India never had. A prominent member of the Indian National Congress, he played a leading role in the struggle for independence and was often imprisoned for his anti-British activities. When it came to the election of the president of the Congress, and de facto prime minister, Gandhi appointed Nehru and forced Patel and J R Kriplani to withdraw their candidacy. A great injustice was done to them in the name of democracy. Patel, the 'Iron Man of India' was made Home Minister in the new government and is remembered as the 'Patron Saint of India's Civil Servants'. He worked tirelessly to maintain the unity of India.

In 2002 his bust was installed in Ealing Road Library, Wembley and in 2018 a statue, the tallest in the world, was erected in Gujarat, amid great controversy because of its unjustifiable and exorbitant cost.

Sarojini Naidu, the first woman to be appointed Governor of a State in India after Independence.

Sarojini Naidu (1879–1949), poet, politician and gifted orator, came to England in 1895 to study at King's College, London, and later at Girton College, Cambridge. Together with Nehru, Patel and others, she became involved in India's fight for freedom. Often imprisoned by the British, she once said that *the specialists think that my heart disease is in an advanced and dangerous state, but I cannot rest till I stir the heart of the world to repentance over the tragedy of martyred India*. Her speech at the Royal Albert Hall in London on 7 November 1919 is acknowledged as one of the best ever made by an Indian in Britain. In 1925 she became President of the Indian National Congress. During the First World War she wrote the following poem:

The Services of Indian Womanhood
Is there aught you need that my hands withhold,
Rich gifts of raiment or grain or gold?
Lo! I have flung to the East and West
Priceless treasures torn of my breast,
And yielded the sons of my stricken womb

To the drum beats of duty, the sabres of doom.
Gathered like pearls in their alien graves,
Silent they sleep by the Persian waves,
Scattered like shells on Egyptian sands
They lie with pale brows and brave, broken hands.
They are strewn like blossoms mown down by chance
On the blood-brown meadows of Flanders and France.
Can ye measure the grief of the tears I weep
Or compass the woe of the watch I keep?
Or the pride that thrills thro' my heart's despair
And the hope that comforts the anguish of prayer,
And the far and glorious vision I see
Of the torn red banners of victory?
When the terror and tumult of hate shall cease
And life be refashioned on anvils of peace,
And your love shall offer memorial thanks
To the comrades who fought in your dauntless ranks,
And you honour the deeds of your deathless ones,
Remember the blood of martyred sons.

Vinayak Damodar Savarkar (1883–1966) was a poet, nationalist and revolutionary who became a national hero, whose magnetic personality, heroism, self-sacrifices and oratory inspired a generation of freedom fighters.

Born near Nasik in Maharashtra, he enrolled at a university in Bombay, but his college attendance was interrupted by his anti-British activities, and he was even asked to leave his hostel. Savarkar came to London to join the Honourable Society of Gray's Inn on a scholarship, helped by Shymaji Krishnavarma. While in residence at India House, he was under constant watch by the authorities. He wanted to fight for independence with revolutionary methods and, in order to do so, founded the Free India Society. His book, *The History of the War of Independence*, was banned throughout the Empire, but he managed to smuggle copies to India to sell by having the names of Charles Dickens and Walter Scott printed on the cover.

Fearful of being arrested in London, Savarkar moved to Bhikaji Cama's house in Paris, but was eventually captured in 1910, given two terms of life imprisonment and put on a boat to India. Risking his life, Savarkar escaped through the porthole of the ship and swam back to France, only to be captured again and imprisoned in India. In 1921 he was released from prison on condition that he renounced his revolutionary activities. Subsequently he travelled the country to promote Hindu nationalism, becoming a great orator; by now his BA degree was withdrawn.

Vinayak Damodar Savarkar.

144

Maulana Abdul Kalam Azad (1888–1958) was a scholar and a senior political leader of the Indian independence movement. As a young man he wrote poetry and became a prominent journalist, writing articles critical of the British rule in India. In 1923, at the age of 35, he became the youngest President of the Indian National Congress and opposed the demand for a separate Muslim state of Pakistan, calling instead for independent India to be committed to secularism. Azad became India's first Minister of Education, emphasising that:

> *'We must not for a moment forget, it is a birth right of every individual to receive at least the basic education without which he cannot fully discharge his duties as a citizen.'*

In 1951, Maulana Azad established the first modern Institute of Technology in India and, on account of his courage and gallantry, came to be described as 'the emperor of learning, a person of the calibre of Plato, Aristotle and Pythagoras'.

Jawaharlal Nehru (1889–1954), writer, lawyer and freedom fighter, was appointed the first Prime Minister of independent India in 1947 by Gandhi. A prominent member of the Indian National Congress, Nehru was imprisoned several times for his anti-British activities, but nevertheless supported the Allied war effort during the Second World War. After independence he embarked on an ambitious programme of economic, social and political reforms. The domination of the Nehru dynasty in politics has not been without criticism.

Maulana Abdul Kalam Azad.

Jawaharlal Nehru.

Dr Bhimrao Ramji Ambedkar (1891–1956) was a jurist, political reformer and human rights activist who campaigned against discrimination of fellow Dalits, known as untouchables. Justice for women and the right to enter Hindu temples and access to public drinking water sources were his other crusades. Dr Ambedkar was awarded a Baroda State scholarship to study at Columbia University in America in 1913 and came to London in 1916 to study at the London School of Economics. He was called to the Bar at Gray's Inn in 1923 after a spell in India. One of the main negotiators for India's independence, Dr Ambedkar was appointed Chairman of the Constitution Drafting Committee in which he emphasised building bridges between castes. He became Independent India's first Minister of Law. In spite of the significant role he played, fighting against injustices in India, and being one of the main authors of the Indian Constitution, Dr Ambedkar has never received the recognition he deserved. His BBC interview in 1955 gives an interesting insight into his views and opinions on Gandhi 'in his human capacity' and not as a Mahatma. He refused to recognise him as such. For him, Gandhi was an orthodox Hindu, an 'episode' and not an 'epoch' maker. In 1951, Ambedkar resigned from the Government.

Dr Bhimrao Ramji Ambedkar.

Rajkumari Amrit Kaur (1889–1964), daughter of Raja Sir Harnam Singh of Kapurthala royal family was described as a living legend who fought for her country and who was often arrested for sedition. An admirer and follower of Gokhale, she devoted her life to serve the country, putting aside the trappings of her privileged up bringing, as did Princesses Sophia and Indira, also from Punjab. After independence, the Rajkumari was appointed the Union Minister of Health, Chairman of the Red Cross and Minister of Sports. She established the Tuberculosis Association of India.

Subhash Chandra Bose (1897–1945) gave up his career in the Civil Service to protest against the massacre at Jallianwalla Bagh. As an activist he demanded complete independence rather than Dominion status within the British Empire and fiercely opposed the Viceroy's declaration of war in 1939 on behalf of India. The Axis powers were seen by him as liberators of India on the basis that 'my enemy's enemy is my friend'. He organised an independent army, the Indian National Army, the Azad Hind, mainly from prisoners of war in Japan, to fight the British in Burma and introduced *Jai Hind*, Hail India as a national salute. Bose became a popular and favourite hero of the independence movement and inspired the youth of the country with the slogan, 'give me your blood and I will give you freedom'. He established a government in exile in Singapore on 21 October 1943. There are now demands for this date to be celebrated as the day of Indian independence instead of 15 August 1947.

Bose did not live to realise his hopes of ruling India. He is supposed to have been badly injured in a plane crash in Taiwan but the controversy about the place and the circumstances of his death are surrounded in mystery, giving rise to conspiracy theories which have become folklore. The most popular belief is that he was taken to

Rajkumari Amrit Kaur.

Subhash Chandra Bose.

Sardar Baldev Singh.

Lakshmi Sahgal.

the local hospital where he died on 18 August 1945, his body cremated and the ashes laid to rest in a temple in Tokyo. His daughter Anita has appealed to the Japanese authorities for the mortal remains of her father to be returned to India. In 2018 the Indian Government released 100 classified files on Bose but the conspiracy theory still continues.

Sardar Baldev Singh (1902–61) represented the Punjab Sikh community and was a leading politician in the Indian independence movement. During the Sir Stafford Cripps Mission of 1942 he took part in the discussions of some form of self-government. He was also a member of the Viceroy's Executive Council. After independence, Baldev Singh became India's first Minister of Defence and a member of the Constituent Assembly of India, and remaining a major political voice on Sikh issues.

Captain Lakshmi Sahgal (1914–2012) officer of the Indian National Army and a right hand woman of Subhash Chandra Bose, was a revolutionary of the Indian Independence movement. She qualified as a doctor from the Madras Medical College in 1938 and practiced in Singapore during World War II, helping the poor as well as the Indian prisoners of war. Having heard about Subhash Chandra Bose, she approached him when he visited Singapore; he told her about his determination to raise a women's regiment to take part in the struggle for independence and gave her a mandate for its formation. Doctor Saghal then became Captain Lakshmi of the Indian National Army and was later arrested by the British for her political activities in the struggle for independence. In 2002 she was selected as a candidate for the Presidential election but was defeated by A P J Abdul Kalam.

CHAPTER 19
Why Britain Gave India Independence

In February 1947, the British Labour Prime Minister, Clement Attlee declared that: *'The present state of uncertainty is fraught with danger and cannot be indefinitely prolonged'* ... *'It is essential that there should be the fullest co-operation with the Indian leaders in all steps that are taken as to the withdrawal of the British power so that the process may go forward as smoothly as possible'.*

Clement Attlee, MP.

1. The most important reason was the strength of the Indian National Army of Subhash Chandra Bose, and its slogans 'Do or Die' and 'Now or Never'. This made the British realise the folly of continuing to resist the demand for independence. There was also widespread unrest in the Indian Armed Forces which made Britain believe they could no longer be trusted. The influence of the 'Quit India' movement, as Attlee stated, was 'minimal'.

2. After the Second World War, Britain could no longer depend on the loyalty of the armed forces in India, especially the Navy, which had hoped that India would be granted independence. In 1946, the ratings of the Royal Indian Navy stopped work and threatened to resign unless their demands were met. Signs of open revolt were crushed, but under such circumstances the British realised they could not keep India under their control for long and decided to withdraw.

3. After the War in 1945, the British authorities decided to try Colonel Shah Nawaz Khan (1914–83), Captain Lakshmi Sehgal (1914–2012), Colonel Gurbaksh Singh Dhillon (1914–2006) and other members of the Indian National Army (the armed force formed by Subhash Chandra Bose and other nationalists in 1942), before a court martial for the crime of waging war against the King-Emperor. All were found guilty and sentenced to transportation for life. Mass demonstrations followed throughout India demanding the release of their heroes, with the result that Field Marshal Auchinleck (1884–1981), Commander-in-Chief of India, granted clemency, and the case against the rest of the accused was withdrawn. There was great rejoicing in the country, confirming to the British government that it was not possible to keep India in chains.

4. The feeling in India that British power and authority were invincible evaporated during the Second World War when British troops struggled at the hands of

the Japanese, proving that Great Britain's position in Asia no longer gave it the strength and influence which for so long had enabled it to rule millions.

5. The Second World War cost Britain so much that it had to borrow enormous sums from America to buy not only raw materials but also basic foodstuffs. When so much energy was required after the war at home to rescue a shattered economy it hardly seemed wise still to be involved with India. In any case, since the Allied powers were fighting for freedom and democracy, the American government put pressure on the British government to grant India independence. Even diehards like Winston Churchill decided there was no advantage in keeping India colonised.

6. Clement Attlee, British Prime Minister in 1945 who had always taken a keen interest in Indian affairs, decided that to keep India in bondage would mean losing the goodwill of its people. Not wishing Indo-British relations to suffer in the long run, and feeling that Britain had much to gain by giving independence to India, he sent Lord Mountbatten to organise the transfer of power.

7. A substantial body of opinion across the world supported India's cause. India's case for freedom was put forward in the Charter of the United Nations, of which Britain was one of the signatories, so it could not talk credibly about freedom for others while keeping India under British rule.

8. Britain's involvement after 1945 in the Cold War between the United States and the Soviet Union was a further factor. The Russians, having an early advantage over the United States, were able to point out to Britain that its situation would improve if it granted independence to India.

9. The concept of the British Commonwealth changed fundamentally. If the British could have other Dominions as members, then there was no reason why India, after independence, could not still be part of it.

10. Maulana Azad felt that, though the British left India, they made sure they continued to have a foothold on the Indian subcontinent through the decision to partition India. As he saw it, it was a policy of 'divide and rule', and a state dominated by the Muslim League would offer Britain a sphere of influence.

11. British soldiers stationed in India during the Second World War gained first-hand experience of the poverty and hardship of the Indian masses, and spoke about it to their friends and relatives on their return home. Such sad observations touched the hearts of the British people and led them to believe that independence might enable the Indians to improve their economic conditions. This explains the unanimous support given by members of parliament to the Indian Independence Bill in July 1947.

CHAPTER 20

Presidents of India

Since India became a Republic on 26 January 1950, and King George VI abandoned the title of Emperor of India, there have been fourteen presidents of the country. Also dubbed 'lords of the realm', they hold office under the Indian Constitution for a five-year term, and are additionally Commander-in-Chief of the Indian armed forces.

The first president elected by the Electoral College was **Dr Rajendra Prasad** (1950–62), the only president to occupy the office for more than two terms. A lawyer who became a political leader, he joined the Indian National Congress during the Indian independence movement.

Sarvepalli Radhakrishnan (1962–67), statesman and philosopher, was the first Vice-President and the second President of India. The first president to make a state visit to Britain in 1963, he was awarded a knighthood in 1931, but declined to use it.

Far left: Dr Rajendra Prasad.

Left: Sarvepalli Radhakrishnan.

Ramaswamy Venkataraman.

Ramaswamy Venkataraman (1987–92), a lawyer and freedom fighter, was the second president to make a state visit to the United Kingdom, in 1990.

Pratibha Patil (2007–12), lawyer and politician, was the only woman president, and the third and last President of India to make a state visit to Britain, in 2009.

Pranab Mukherjee, (2012–17). He came to office decades after a political career as a senior member of the Indian National Congress.

Ram Nath Kovind, was elected President in 2017, he was Governor of Bihar from 2015–17 and a Member of Parliament from 1994–2006.

Queen Elizabeth II has paid three visits to India as Head of the Commonwealth of Nations. The first was in 1961, when Dr Rajendra Prasad was President. In 1983, she went to India to attend the 8th Commonwealth Heads of Government Meeting, when Zail Singh was the President. Her last visit was in 1997, when K R Narayanan was the President of India: she visited the Jallianwalla Bagh and laid a wreath at the site of the Amritsar massacre of 1919.

Pratibha Patil.

Pranab Mukherjee.

Ram Nath Kovind.

HRH Queen Elizabeth II.

CHAPTER 21

The Legacy of British Rule in India – Good and Bad

After ruling for nearly 200 years, the British left India in 1947 with a mixed legacy. Alongside the many positive benefits of the Raj came also some of the most unacceptable and unforgivable atrocities with which they controlled India for their own economic advantages. Their positive deeds in India are as rewarding as their acts of cruelty are, ultimately, unpardonable. Although they went to India for trade and not for territory, the British ended up as conquerors, and transformed India into a colony. They exploited the territory as a major source of raw materials and investments for their financial gains. The British took more away than they gave, reaping enormous profits at India's expense and putting vast numbers of the population into a state of extreme poverty. The country was systematically drained of capital resources.

Equally, British scholars, scientists, administrators and even politicians have enriched India, and changed the course of history, for a better and united country. They established institutes for education and scientific and artistic organisations. Best of all, they introduced the system of law and administration and re-discovered India's past.

After independence, in the interest of harmonious Indo-British relations, India asked for neither apology nor reparations from the British for all their misdeeds and maltreatment of the people.

Independent India's system of administration was handed over wholesale by the British, with special manuals prepared for every government department, containing detailed instructions regarding its efficient functioning. A system of competitive examination was introduced for India's Civil Service.

It was British imperialism that brought about the unification of the country and, most important of all, a sense of belonging to one nation, that gave rise to national consciousness. However, the British took advantage of different religious groups in the country, maximising their efforts to interfere in the relationship between Hindus and Muslims by means of undermining each other's strength in order to consolidate their power. This policy of Divide and Rule eventually led to the partition of India.

The first passenger train service ran from Bombay to Thane in 1853. By 1880 a network of over 9000 miles connected the interior to the three major port cities of Bombay, Calcutta and Madras.

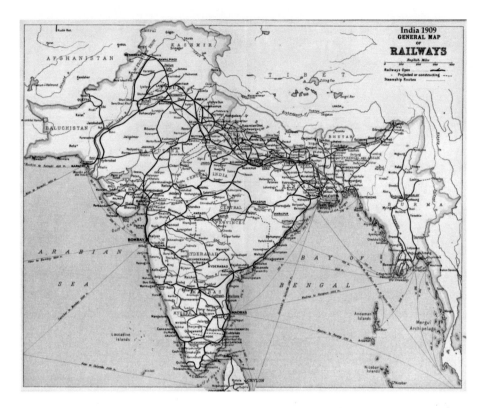

Industrialisation of India was paid for by British investment, especially in the railways, to mobilize the military in the country and for commercial purposes, for transporting cotton and other raw materials with speed and ease to the ports for export to Britain. The network of railways, connecting every corner of the country, and becoming the largest employer in the world, benefited India enormously. But the same could not be said when it came to shipping the cargo to Britain. The British decided to use their own ships only, which affected the Indian shipping industry very badly.

The suppressed growth of industries also set back the Indian economy at least 100 years behind that of the West. British imperialism resulted in social, economic and moral stagnation. In the major cities, large numbers of landowners were ruined by the policy of auctioning off the right of revenue collection to the highest bidder.

The urbanisation of the country, with factories built by the British all over India, revolutionised family and social life. Villagers were drawn to the cities for work, causing housing problems and giving rise to the slums.

For the adoption of their democratic, parliamentary form of government and legal system in an independent India, credit must go to the British. Perhaps the most important legacy of all was the rule of law. No punishment was allowed except according to the law, which applied equally to Hindus, Muslims, Sikhs, Christians,

Buddhists and Zoroastrians. The legal system in India is still based on the analytical system, just as it is in Britain. The seminal text *Jurisprudence* by Salmond is taught equally in India as in Britain.

But the law was differently executed when it came to punishments meted out to Indian and British culprits: accused of the same crime, generally, the Briton got away with a caution, whilst the Indian was put into prison.

The British set up institutions of higher learning in India, replacing the *pathshalas* and *madrassas* with high schools, colleges and universities. The introduction of the English language brought with it an exposure to English literature. The art of writing novels was very much influenced by examples in English, while British principles of literary criticism were also adopted in India. Even Indian drama was much inspired by English theatre. The same can be said of newspapers: started by the British for themselves, they came in time to be published by Indians in English and various Indian languages. The British initially imposed press censorship to prevent discussions of subjects likely to affect the authority of the government, although this was later repealed.

It was the British who re-discovered India's past, deciphering Brahmi script and making it possible to decrypt inscriptions in other parts of the country, especially on the Ashoka pillars. The British studied Sanskrit and translated the bulk of Buddhist literature, in particular the *Vedas*. They also documented the history of ancient India; the five volumes of the *Cambridge History of India* are a much treasured legacy.

Although the East India Company was against missionary activity in its territorial possessions, in 1813, under pressure, it reluctantly allowed missionaries to travel in its ships. The preachers' propaganda and criticism of native faiths made Hindus re-examine the ideology of their religion and they, in turn, were influenced by western concepts. Raja Ram Mohan Roy, a scholar who admired Christianity, was ready to borrow everything that was good in it, as 'India's Columbus in the discovery of a new continent of truth'. He believed in the understanding and bonding of eastern and western cultures.

It is true that the more regrettable aspects of the legacy of the Raj cannot be overlooked. Any official apology from the British, for the Mutiny of 1857, the 1919 Jallianwalla Bagh massacre or the man-made Bengal famine of 1942, is long overdue and would be very much appreciated. However, despite these unforgivable British misdeeds, there is nevertheless today great appreciation of, and gratitude for, its beneficial and long-lasting influence in India, not least the English language and English law.

Of course, the positive effects of the Indo-British relationship have not been one-sided: the British gained greatly from their rule of India, without which Great Britain would never have become the superpower it is today.

There is much to celebrate about the combined history of India and Britain and their unique relationship.

CHAPTER 22

Pukka Job: Indian Words Adopted into the English Language

When traders from England went to India in 1591 they set foot in a land with a different culture, different climate and totally different language. English of the 17th century was the language of Shakespeare, and foreign words were not readily accepted, except Latin and French, but in the subsequent 400 years the linguistic relationship between the two countries has grown with trade. While they may not have got used to the culture and the climate, the English accepted no fewer than 900 Indian words into their vocabulary.

At the height of the Moghul Empire, many Indian words linked with trade and objects were adopted into the English language. Baksheesh, bazaar, brinjal, bungalow, calico, chintz, cha, chokidar, cot, dhoti, dingy, dungaree, durbar, guru, godown, hookah, juggernaut, munshi, palanquin, pariah, sahib, shampoo, shawl and yogi, are amongst many in common use. The word 'mogul' itself was adopted by the English to mean 'a great personage or an autocratic ruler'.

Following the words dealing with commerce, the 18th century saw the assimilation of words like avatar, ayah, baboo, buggy, jungle, jute, loot and seersucker.

The 19th century saw a further increase in word combinations, for example, cot-bed, khaki-clad, and hybrids such as gymkhana, cummerbund, memsahib and competition-wallah. The terms 'civil service' and 'red tape' are not Indian, but originated in India.

The usage of Indian words by the English continued to evolve in a fascinating way. In contrast to the words used in commerce, there now followed the introduction of words with political and military connections, such as sepoy, subedar, jamadar and havildar.

The new relationship between India and England gave rise to the word 'Indo-Europe' for the first time. 'Think what the syntheses of these two words, Indian and Europe, implies,' the German Indologist Max Müller (1823–1900) was prompted to reflect: 'Nothing has drawn the bonds of fellowship between India and England more closely than this discovery of the common origin of their language and of principal languages of Europe, and more particularly England.'

In the 20th century, during the Indian struggle for independence, words like ahimsa, Blighty, hartal, swaraj and satyagrah appeared in newspaper headlines. By the time of the First and Second World Wars, ek dum, goonda, zoolm, chup, izzat and jaldee-jaldee became familiar and popular descriptions for giving orders and describing wrongdoers.

Eminent English writers have used Indian words in their work with great ease. During the time of Elizabeth I, India was a distant land of wonder, wealth, diamonds and elephants. Dr John Fryer (b. *c*.1733), who wrote *A New Account of East India and Persia*, used the words maharaja, peshwa, pundits and rajaship. Perhaps the most interesting use of Indian words in the legal profession was when Edmund Burke – who never went to India – prosecuting Warren Hastings for corruption, assured the tribunal that 'the Indian vocabulary will, by degrees, become familiar to your lordships, as we develope the modes and customs of the country.'

Many eminent writers used Indian words with scholarly ability and accuracy. Charles Lamb used banyan-day; Jane Austen used mohur, nabob, and palanquin; Thomas More wrote of amrita and vina; Charles Dickens mentioned divan, fakir, jungle, loot, pugree, punch, shampoo and verandah. Sir Walter Scott wrote *The Surgeon's Daughter*, the first English novelist to take up an Indian theme when 'the Honourable East India Company in Leadenhall Street were silent laying the foundation of that immense empire, which afterwards rose like an exhalation'. Both Thackeray and Kipling made lavish use of Indian words, as did E M Forster.

The English who went to India as 'illegal immigrants' remained in the minority of the population and adopted less than a thousand Indian words into English. By contrast, the Indians have taken the English language as their own. India is governed through communication in English, making it the 'national' language of the country. Most educated Indians speak English as their mother tongue. And yet, when a Briton speaks an Indian language, it becomes a matter of great surprise.

CHAPTER 23

Burials and Cremations of Notable Indians in Britain

Cremation was against the law in Britain until Sir Henry Thomson, surgeon to Queen Victoria, founded the Cremation Society of England in 1874. But it was not until 1885 that the first cremation took place, in Woking, after a period of establishing legal formalities and the best way of cremating a body. One experiment in 1879 was the cremation of a horse to see how quickly and completely it was reduced to ashes.

All those who died in England before 1885 were buried, whatever their religion, hence the internment of the first Indian to be buried in Britain, **Raja Ram Mohan Roy** (1774–1833), who died in Bristol. According to his wishes, he was buried in a corner of the garden of the house where he died. On a pilgrimage to his burial place, Raja's friend Dwarkanath Tagore decided to create a suitable monument to him. As a result his remains were removed and reinterred in Arnos Vale Cemetery, Bristol. *The Times* obituary for Roy read as follows: *His talents and acquirements were great; he wrote and spoke English with ease and accuracy and even elegance, but about his whole*

The Raja Ram Mohan Roy chhatri in Arnos Vale Cemetary, Bristol.

Dwarkanath Tagore, and his tomb in Kensal Green Cemetery.

Memorial to Jind Kaur, the Maharani of Punjab, dedicated by her son, Maharaja Duleep Singh, in Kensal Green Cemetery, London.

demeanour there was a charm of modesty and reverence that produced the most agreeable effect on all who saw or conversed with him. A more remarkable man has not distinguished modern times and advance of opinion.

Dwarkanath Tagore (1794–1846), industrialist, benefactor and grandfather of Rabindranath Tagore, the poet laureate, was the second Indian to be buried in England. He had worked in partnership with British traders and often visited England, and used to say that 'the happiness of India is best secured by her connection with England'. He died in Brown's Hotel in London and was buried in Kensal Green Cemetery. There was no religious service at the funeral, but his heart was removed and taken to Calcutta, where it was cremated with full Brahmo rites. Since he had been received by Queen Victoria and Prince Albert like an 'old friend', they sent four carriages for the funeral to ensure a princely send-off. In his obituary, the London *Daily Mail* wrote: *Descended from the highest Brahmin caste of India, his family can prove a long and undoubted pedigree. But it is not on account of this nobility that we now review his life but on far better grounds. However gifted, his claims rest on a higher pedestal – he was the benefactor of his country...*

H H The Maharaja Sir Nripendra of Cooch Behar (1862–1911), Honorary ADC to King Edward VII (1901–11), was the first Maharaja to be cremated at Golders Green Crematorium, London, opened in 1902. The main chapel displays a commemorative plaque for him and his two heirs, Rajendra and Jitendra Narayan. On the wall opposite is a bust of Sir Henry Thomson, the founder of the Cremation Society.

H H The Maharaja Sir Nripendra of Cooch Behar.

Right: Plaques to (left) H H Maharaja Rai Rajendra Narayan Bhup Bahadur of Cooch Behar, (centre) to H H the Maharaja Sir Nripendra of Cooch Bihar, (right) Maharaja Sir Jitendra Narayan of Cooch Bihar.

Below: Photo of The Maharaja Sir Jitendra Narayan of Cooch Behar, adjacent to the plaques.

Jamsetji Tata.

Freddie Mercury (1946–91) of Queen was cremated at Kensal Green Cemetery. His plaque, in French, translates as: *In Loving Memory of Farrokh Bulsara, 5 Sept. 1946– 24 Sept. Nov. 1991. Always To Be Close To You With All My Love. M.*

Brookwood Cemetery, Woking, Surrey was opened in 1854 and is the largest cemetery in Britain. The first crematorium in Britain was also built at Woking in 1879. Indian Muslim soldiers who died in the First World War are buried here and, according to military tradition, the headstones marking their final resting places are laid in straight rows, to indicate soldiers on parade.

Jamsetji Tata (1839–1904), industrialist and founder of the TATA Group, is buried in the cemetery among other notable Indian philanthropists, industrialists, politicians and diplomats who made their mark in the history of India and Britain. He established India's biggest conglomerate company and is regarded as 'the father of Indian industry'. Following his death, Lord Curzon, the Viceroy of India said that, 'No Indian of the present generation had done more for the commerce industry in India'.

Sir Ratanji Tata (1871–1918), younger son of Jamsetji and an industrialist and philanthropist interested in the welfare of the poor, was buried beside his father.

Sir Dorabji Tata (1859–1932), industrialist and educator, and the older son of Jamsetji Tata, died in Germany and was buried at Brookwood. The Dorabji Mausoleum next to that of his father is an outstanding building with classical Egyptian and Persian features.

Far left: Shapurji Saklatvala addressing a rally in Trafalgar Square.

Centre: Monument to philanthropist Ghanshyam Das Birla in Golders Green Crematorium.

Left: Azim Husain.

Sir Mancherjee Merwanjee Bhownagree (1851–1933), the second Indian Member of Parliament at Westminster, is buried in Brookwood Cemetery.

Shapurji Saklatvala (1874–1936), the third Indian elected to Parliament at Westminster, was the son of Jamsetji Tata's sister. He was cremated at Golders Green Crematorium, and his ashes were buried at Brookwood.

Ghanshyam Das Birla (1894–1983) industrialist and philanthropist inherited the family business. Later he established a jute factory and invested in tea and textiles through a series of acquisitions from European companies. He was a life-long freedom fighter and died in London. There is a life-size statue of him, overlooking the gardens at Golders Green Crematorium in London. The inscription reads, *What we call life, is a wonderful journey, full of purpose. When the mission is realised the person passes away. This is the eternal law of nature.*

Sir Mancherjee Merwanjee Bhownagree.

Azim Husain (1913–2007), relinquished his inheritance in Pakistan after partition to remain in India. He was a negotiator during the Partition riots and became India's most distinguished diplomat, being appointed Deputy High Commissioner in London and Ambasador to Egypt and Switzerland. Internationally, he put forward India's objections to the Non-Nuclear Proliferation Treaty at the United Nations. He is buried at Brookwood Cemetery near his brother Naim, who died in 1931 during his student days at Cambridge. His father was a member of the Viceroy's cabinet.

Since 1968, the Crematorium, Golder's Green, London has a large brass OM for Hindu funeral services donated by the author in memory of her father, WWI auxiliary and social reforms writer, Maganlal Premji Vadgama (1895–1963).

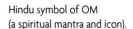

Hindu symbol of OM (a spiritual mantra and icon).

CHAPTER 24

Remembered and Recognised

Trafalgar Square – the link with India

Trafalgar Square in the centre of London is as much a part of Indian history as it is of British history. While the larger-than-life-size statue of Viscount Horatio Nelson (1758–1805) is a fitting memorial to his victory against the combined fleet of France and Spain in 1805 at Trafalgar, the two statues on the two southern corners of the square are in honour of British victories in India.

One is of Sir Charles Napier (1782–1853), a General of the British Empire who was sent to India in 1842 with orders to put down the rebels in the Sindh province. But he greatly exceeded his mandate and conquered the whole province. To announce his victory back in England he is supposed to have sent the shortest message ever: *Peccavi* – Latin for 'I have sinned'. But that is just folklore. In fact the real author of

Right: The two statues in the southern corners of Trafalgar Square, commemorating General Charles Napier (right) and Major-General Sir Henry Havelock (far right).

the message was a teenager, Catherine Winkworth (1827–78), who sent it as a joke in 1844 to the new satirical magazine *Punch*. A clever example of the British sense of humour, the pun was wrongfully credited to Napier.

Napier annexed Sindh, was made Governor, and created a police force there, the best in India. His statue bears a scroll, symbolic of the administration of Sindh. Years later, however, Napier was to refer to his conquest of Sindh as a 'harsh and barbarous aggression.' 'Our objective of conquering India, as the object of all our cruelties,' he wrote in his diary, 'was money ... every shilling of this has been picked out of blood, wiped and put into the missellers' pocket ... we shall yet suffer for the crime as sure as there is God in Heaven.'

The other statue commemorates Sir Henry Havelock (1795–1857), who studied at Middle Temple and went to India in 1823. He spoke Persian and Hindi and became a Baptist. During the Indian Mutiny of 1857, he guarded the garrison at Cawnpore and Lucknow and defeated the sepoys four times. Havelock was knighted and created a Baron.

In the past there have been strong demands for the two statues to be either relocated or demolished, on the grounds that historically there is nothing to celebrate about their actions in India. Whatever the arguments, removing the statues will not remove the facts of history, however unpleasant and unacceptable.

Blue plaques

'Blue plaques', as they are popularly known, are ornamental, circular plaques installed by English Heritage (now known as Historic England) or, unofficially, by local authorities or other public bodies, to mark a property where an eminent person lived or worked. They are inscribed with the name of the person, the dates of the period during which they lived in that building and their contribution – Poet, Noble Laureate, Social Reformer, Campaigner for India's independence, etc. They are lasting monuments to particular individuals who may only have occupied the premises for a short period, but their names live on. Out of the 1,800 plaques in London commemorating the lives of men and women who have left their mark on society, 18 are for Indian men but none for Indian women.

Ali Mohammad Abbas (1922–79), Pakistani lawyer and politician, lived at 33 Tavistock Square, WC1, in 1945, before partition. He called his flat 'Pakistan House' as a base for the All-India Muslim League, of which he was secretary. A noted public speaker, he was the first Asian barrister to appear at all levels of the English legal system.

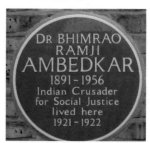

Dr Bhimrao Ramji Ambedkar (1891–1956), politician, lived at King Henry's Road, NW3, whilst a student at the London School of Economics (1916–23). He campaigned against the Indian caste system and made a greater single contribution to

the drafting of the Indian constitution than any other individual. He was appointed Law Minister when India became independent in 1947. There is a bust of Dr Ambedkar, as well as a portrait, in the London School of Economics.

Nirad C Chaudhuri (1897–1999), who lived at 20 Lathbury Road, Oxford, is best known for his book, *The Autobiography of an Unknown Indian*. His dedication in the book praising the Raj, caused controversy in the newly independent India.

Born in Bengal, Chaudhuri worked as a journalist and an editor for various publications in India, and came to Oxford in the mid '50s, never to return to India. A prolific writer, he continued publishing several books, gaining popularity and admiration from his readers.

Mohandas Karamchand Gandhi (1869–1948), lawyer and politician, lived at 20 Barons Court, West Kensington, when he came to England in 1888 at the age of 19 to study law at the Inner Temple. His dislike for his landlady's meat dishes led him to join the Theosophical Society in order to remain a vegetarian. There is a second plaque to Gandhi at Kingsley Hall, Powis Road, Bow, where he stayed when he came to London in 1931 for the Second Round Table Conference.

Sri Aurobindo Ghosh (1872–1950), politician and spiritual leader, lived at 49 St Stephen's Avenue, W12 from 1884 to 1887 when he attended St Paul's School in Hammersmith. He devoted his life to spiritual activities and after early involvement with the nationalist movement created a new philosophy of 'integral yoga'. *The Times*, in its Literary Supplement of 1944, said of him that 'to study his writings is to enlarge the boundaries of one's knowledge... He is a yogi who writes as though he were standing among stars, with the constellations for his companions'.

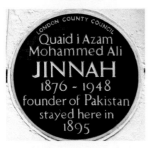

Quaid i Azam, Mohammed Ali Jinnah (1876–1948), lived at 35 Russell Road, West Kensington, in 1895, a year before he joined the Indian National Congress, believing at that time in a united India. On becoming President of the All-India Muslim League in 1916, he changed his stance, supporting a separate Muslim state, and became the founder of Pakistan.

Sir Syed Ahmed Khan (1817–98), Indian reformer and educationalist, lived at 21 Mecklenburg Square, WC1, from 1869 to 1870. During the Mutiny of 1857 he came to the help of Britons in danger, but later wrote a book criticising the British rule in India. A member of the Muslim community, he campaigned for a two-nation future for the subcontinent.

Krishna Menon (1896–1974), Indian politician, diplomat and St Pancras Councillor (1934–1947), was, for a long time, the voice of India in Britain. A brown Camden Borough Council plaque marks his house at 57 Camden Square NW1, from where he helped Allen Lane found the Penguin publishing house. An English Heritage blue plaque was unveiled in 2013, at 30 Langton Park Road N6 where he lived from 1929–31, in recognition of his distinguished statesmanship. In 1947 he was appointed independent India's first High Commissioner to the United Kingdom; later becoming the Indian Ambassador to the United Nations (1952–62).

Jawaharlal Nehru (1889–1964), politician, lived at 60 Elgin Crescent, Notting Hill, while studying at the Inner Temple (1910–12). He took up politics and campaigned for Indian independence, spending periodic spells in prison. He became India's first Prime Minister (1947–64) and leader of the Third World non-aligned movement.

Sardar Vallabhbhai Javerbhai Patel (1875–1950), Indian statesman, lived at 23 Aldridge Villas, Westbourne Grove, while a student at the Middle Temple (1912–14). He was the leader of India's freedom movement and, after independence in 1947, became the first Home Secretary as well as the Deputy Prime Minister.

Raja Ram Mohan Roy (1772–1833), social reformer and the prophet of modern India, lived at 49 Bedford Square, Bloomsbury. He fought for the rights of women and the abolition of the rituals of *suttee* and child marriage. He was the first Indian to come on an official visit to England, in 1831, as an envoy of the Moghul Emperor Akbar II, to complain about the East India Company. He was presented to King William IV and given a seat of honour at his coronation.

Vinayak Damodar Savarkar (1883–1966), philosopher, Indian revolutionary and politician, lived at 65 Cromwell Avenue, N6 in 1906, whilst a law student. A committed patriot, he held views more extreme than those of the Indian National Congress. In 1910 he was sentenced to 50 years in prison for his revolutionary activities, but was released in 1921, falsely assuring the authorities that he would 'give it all up'. In 1924 he was back in jail, remaining there until 1937. After his release he joined the Hindu Mahasabha and became its President.

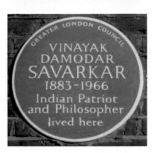

P C Kulwant Sidhu (1975–99), a police officer, died when he fell through a glass panel on the roof of a commercial building on Mereway Road, Twickenham. The incident happened when he was chasing two suspected burglars on the night of 25 October 1999. His bravery is recognised by the Police Memorial Trust.

The Maharaja Duleep Singh (1838–93), a member of the Indian royalty, lived at 54 Holland Park, W11, from 1881 to 1886. He came to the throne at the age of five when his father, Maharaja Ranjit Singh, died. In 1849 he was deposed and brought to England as a ward of Queen Victoria. The Maharaja's attempts to reclaim his state in India failed and he lived most of his life in Britain. The world famous Koh-i-Noor diamond, owned by his father, was part of the loot that the British took away.

Rabindranath Tagore (1861–1941), poet, philosopher, and the first Asian Nobel Laureate, lived at 3 Villa on the Heath, Vale of Health, in 1912. His poems, collected in *Gitanjali*, (1910), were translated into English. Playwright, short story writer, painter and philosopher, he also composed the Indian national anthem.

Lokmanaya Tilak (1856–1920), Indian patriot and philosopher, lived at 10 Howley Place, Little Venice (1918–19). Tilak brought a court case against Sir Valentine Chirol, the foreign editor of *The Times*, for making libellous comments about him in his book, *Indian Unrest*, calling Tilak 'the father of the Indian Unrest'. Tilak lost the case; the judge summed up by saying, 'A man twice convicted of sedition has no character to lose'.

Swami Vivekananda (1863–1902), philosopher, stayed at 63 St George's Drive, SW1, in 1896. He came to the West to promote Indian philosophy and inter-faith awareness, and was the first Indian to promote Hinduism to the status of a world religion. In Chicago in 1893, at the Parliament of World Religions, he explained Hinduism with the clear message that 'I do not come to convert you to a new belief. I want you to keep your own belief. I want to teach you to live the truth, to reveal the light within your own soul.' Newspapers of the time praised him as 'the greatest figure in Parliament'. When Vivekananda visited England in 1895 and 1896, he met Max Müller, the noted Indologist from Oxford University, and returned to India with three English disciples, Captain and Mrs Sevier and J J Goodwin, mission accomplished, having spoken to western audiences on the antiquity and beauty of ancient Indian civilisation.

Indian Freemen of British Cities

Bestowal of the honour of the Freedom of the City is one of the oldest British traditions dating back to 1237 and is closely linked to the membership of the City of London Livery Companies. The prestigious award is a unique part of the history of the City, open by nomination only, to highly regarded members of society, visiting dignitaries and statesmen, in recognition of their achievements.

The symbolic ceremony and presentation of the valuable document, written on parchment, have remained unchanged for centuries.

In 1855 Sir Jamsetjee Jeejeebhoy became the first Indian in Britain to receive the Freedom of the City London for his philanthropic work.

Other Indians to follow him, all men, are:

1876   Sir Salar Jung, Prime Minister to the Nizam of Hyderabad, London

1917   Sir Satyendra Prasana Sinha, Executive Councillor of Bengal, London

1919   His Highness Maharaja Sir Ganga Singh, Bahadur of Bikaner, London

1921   His Highness Maharaja Dhiraj Mirza, Maharao Shri Khengarji Savai Bahadur, Maharao of Kutch, London

1921   Rt Hon Sir V S Srinivasan Sastri, Politician, London and Edinburgh

1926   Sir Bijoy Chand Mahtab, Maharaja of Burdwan, Stoke-on-Trent, Edinburgh and Manchester

1931   Hamidullah Khan, Nawab of Bhopal, London

1935   Bhupinder Singh, Maharaja of Patiala, Edinburgh

1957   Jawarhalal Nehru, Prime Minister of India, London

2015   Lord Bahttacharyya, Academic, Coventry

2015   Ratan Tata, Chairman Tata & Sons, Coventry

2016   Lord Parekh, Academic, Kingston-upon-Hull

2017   Pankaj Vadgama, Academic, London

2017   Yashvardhan Kumar Sinha, Indian High Commissioner, London

2017   Kishan Devani, Arts, London

CHAPTER 25

Memorials, Mansions and Monuments

What the British could not carry back with them to Britain, they re-created in buildings and monuments all around the country in the style and spirit of Indian architecture.

The Royal Pavilion, popularly known as the Brighton Pavilion (see p.41), is a former Royal residence built between 1787 and 1822, a most exotic building that has become the emblem of the south coast town of Brighton. From the outside it looks very Indian, while its interior is a mixture of Chinese and Indian design. During the First World War the Pavilion was converted into a military hospital for wounded Indian soldiers, as were the adjacent Dome and Corn Exchange. Three separate kitchens catered for meat-eating Muslims, meat-eating Hindus and vegetarians. Three years after the end of the war, a new gateway to the Pavilion was unveiled by His Highness Maharaja of Patiala, a gift from its princes to serve as a permanent memorial to the nearly 28,000 men from the region who lost their lives in the war.

The 53 Indian soldiers who died of their wounds in the makeshift hospital in Brighton were cremated on the Downs nearby, and the spot where their souls ascended is now marked by a permanent memorial, the **Chhatri**, unveiled by the Prince of Wales in 1921 in the presence of the Maharaja of Patiala. 'in grateful admiration and brotherly affection'.

Below: The Indian Memorial Gateway to the Royal Pavilion, Brighton.

Right: The Chhatri on the Sussex Downs near Brighton.

Above left: Britain's first mosque, the Shah Jahan Mosque in Woking, Surrey built in 1889.

Above: The obelisk at Barton-on-Sea, Hampshire commemorating the injured Indian soldiers who convalesced in the town.

Purely Indian in appearance, the Chhatri was designed by a brilliant young Indian architect, E C Henriques. It bears the inscription: *'To the memory of all the Indian soldiers who gave their lives for the King-Emperor in the Great War, this monument, erected on the site of the funeral pyre where the Hindus and the Sikhs who died in the hospital at Brighton passed through the fire, is in grateful admiration and brotherly affection dedicated.'*

Wounded Muslim Indian soldiers who succumbed to their injuries were buried in a special Muslim cemetery built in 1915 at Horsell Commons, Woking, in the vicinity of Britain's first mosque, the **Shah Jahan Mosque**, built in 1889 and opened by Begum Bhopal. In 1968, their remains, including one Hindu and one unidentified body, were exhumed from the Memorial Gardens, Woking and reinterred in the nearby Military Section in Brookwood Cemetery. The Indo-Saracenic-style domed entrance to the Muslim cemetery still stands 'as a reminder of the sacrifice and its association with the Eastern World'.

Hundreds of Indian soldiers convalesced in huts built along the seafront at **Barton-on-Sea**. An obelisk commemorates their stay under the care of the army doctors, and carries the inscription: *'This memorial is erected to commemorate the establishment at Barton-on-Sea in 1914 of the Convalescent Depot for Indian Troops who fought in Europe during the Great War and was subscribed for by members of the staff.'*

In the **Indian Army Memorial Room** at the Royal Military Academy at Sandhurst are stained glass windows immortalising Indian soldiers, unveiled in 1971 by Field Marshal Sir Claude Auchinleck.

Stained glass windows in the Indian Army Memorial Room at the Royal Military Academy at Sandhurst.

A floor **plaque to the Women's Auxiliary Corps in India, 1942–47**, was unveiled in St Paul's Cathedral in 1971 by HM Queen Elizabeth II. See overleaf.

The Commonwealth Memorial Gates on Constitution Hill, London, commemorate the Armed Forces of the British Empire in the two World Wars. They were funded by lottery money and were unveiled by Her Majesty the Queen in 2002, in the Golden Jubilee of her reign, 57 years after the end of the Second World War. The long overdue decision to recognise the courage and sacrifices of the fallen heroes with a memorial was an idea first mooted by the author.

The four pillars with bronze urns on top, are carved with the names of the countries, continents and territories of the Empire – India, Pakistan, Bangladesh, Sri Lanka, Nepal, Africa and the Caribbean. The names of the holders of the Victoria Cross and the George Cross are listed on the ceiling of the Chhatri.

Unfortunately, unlike any memorial elsewhere in the world, these Memorial Gates are a monument to those who built them rather than for those who gave their lives for the freedom of a country not their own. The names of the Patron, the

Far left: Floor plaque in St Paul's Cathedral, London, dedicated to the Women's Auxiliary Corps in India, 1942–47. Above this in St Paul's Cathedral is the panel dedicated to the Indian and Gurkha soldiers of the Indian Army 1746–1947 (left).

Below: Commonwealth Memorial Gates.

Chairman, the Trustees, the architect, the contractor and the stonemason are prominently positioned in the forefront. By contrast, the names of the war heroes, in whose honour the Gates were built, are tucked away on the ceiling of the Chhatri, out of sight. It is even difficult to fathom the inscription on the Gates, 'Our future is greater than our past', which has no relevance to the fallen heroes. The Memorial lacks awe and the power to move emotionally, unlike the Chhatri on the Brighton Downs and The Cenotaph in Whitehall, London. Instead it seeks equality of greatness of its constructors with the supreme sacrifices of the soldiers.

During the planning period, the author was invited by Baroness Flather, the Chairman of the Memorial Gates Trust to join the Committee. It was a short lived association and the end came when objection was raised by the author against the names of the Patron, Trustees, The Chairman and others being inscribed on the Gates. In response to the author's letter of resignation, Lord Bernard Weatherill, a

Top: Stained glass window at St Luke's Church, Radcilffe Square, London, donated by Sir Mancherji Bhownagree in memory of his sister.

Above: Plinth in Bethnal Green, London, to commemorate the 60th year of Queen Victoria's reign. Presented by Sir Mancherjee Bhownagree.

Trustee, personally telephoned her to discuss the matter because, 'we cannot do without you'. A welcome meeting and amicable discussion took place in Parliament in the presence of Viscount Slim but, sadly the wrong names still found their way on to the Gates.

It has been a matter of great sadness that the contribution to the British war effort by the Empire, and especially India, was never considered worthy of receiving official gratitude from the British Government. Not only were the Memorial Gates built much too late but only through the efforts of private enthusiasts. A great injustice is done by Britain to the people of the then Empire for not honouring them with a monument on behalf of the nation.

However it is not too late, even after the centenary of the First World War, for Britain to right the wrongs of paying tribute to the Indian soldiers, if after all this time, a statue of the first Indian to be awarded the Victoria Cross, Khudadad Khan, could be erected in London as a way of saying 'Thank you' on behalf of the nation.

The Memorial in Whitehall, London, honouring the services of women in World War II, was unveiled by Queen Elizabeth II in 2005 as part of the 60th anniversary of the end of the war, but it is noticeable that the uniform-sari is completely omitted from the uniforms sculpted on the Memorial. The absence of Indian women veterans present for the unveiling ceremony was regrettable.

The annual Festival of Remembrance at the Royal Albert Hall, organised by The Royal British Legion has also never acknowledged the contribution of Indian and Empire soldiers in the Great War, giving a false impression that Britain won the war without their involvement. The ignored soldiers from the Empire do not even constitute a footnote in the event. These brave service men and women who served and died for a country not their own, are treated as mere spectators in the British victory. For the last three years, the author has appealed, without much success, to right this wrong. In 2018, for the first time in its history, there was a passing reference to Commonwealth soldiers forming part of the British armed forces. No further details of individual countries or of their huge contribution were mentioned. A parade of flags of the Commonwealth countries simply registered their presence in the war. It is ironic that while the Empire soldiers volunteered to sacrifice their lives, they still have to beg for recognition.

Raja Ram Mohan Roy Chhatri, Arnos Vale Cemetery, Bristol. The social reformer Raja Ram Mohan Roy, died in Bristol in 1833 and was first buried at Stapleton, but then reinterred at Arnos Vale in 1843. A mausoleum, based on the design of a Bengali Chhatri, was later built over his grave, now a Grade II listed monument. A miniature ivory bust was placed inside, and a book of condolences was kept in the lodge of the cemetery for his friends to sign. It remains an important place of pilgrimage for people from all over the world to pay tribute to the prophet of modern India. There is also a statue of Raja Ram Mohan Roy in the city.

Left: Daylesford House, Gloucestershire.

Below left: Sezincote House, Gloucestershire.

Daylesford House in Gloucestershire was acquired in 1788 by Warren Hastings, who had it remodelled to the design of Samuel Pepys Cockerell with magnificent classical and Indian decoration. The picturesque Anglo-Indian-style building was furnished with rich oriental fabrics and exquisite furniture carved with solid ivory. The house was full of oriental souvenirs and mementoes Warren Hastings brought back from India.

Sezincote House in Gloucestershire, built in 1805, is a stunning example of Indian architecture. The site was purchased by Colonel John Cockerell, grandson of the diarist Samuel Pepys, on his return from India, and the mansion designed by his architect brother Samuel Pepys Cockerell. It has a Neo-Moghul-style dome, complemented by minarets, peacock-tail windows, jali work railings, a pavilion and a Hindu temple in the park. An Indian influence is also seen in the garden, with two statues of elephants and two cast-iron bulls over the bridge. In the Second World War Sezincote House was used as temporary accommodation for Canadian troops.

Elveden Hall in Elveden, Suffolk, was purchased by Maharaja Duleep Singh in 1863. He redesigned the interior to resemble the fine palaces he had been accustomed to in his childhood in India. The mansion played host to a whole range of sporting activities, especially shooting. After his death in 1893, Elveden Hall was bought by Edward Cecil Guinness, the 1st of Earl of Iveagh.

The Durbar Hall at Osborne House, Queen Victoria's holiday house on the Isle of Wight, has a special room to display all her gifts from India, in particular for her Golden Jubilee and Diamond Jubilee in 1887 and 1897. Built for state functions, it houses copper vases, Indian armour and a model of an Indian palace, as well as a collection of paintings of Maharajas and princes, and caskets containing loyal greetings from India. The walls are decorated with Indian symbols, including the Hindu god Ganesh.

The Maharaja's Well at Stoke Row, Henley-on-Thames in Oxfordshire is a unique monument in the English landscape with a touch of Indian mystique. For over 150 years this historic, ornate, if not a little out of place superstructure has attracted a great deal of attention. The story of the well is as fascinating as its exotic design.

The Maharaja of Banaras's aide, E A Reade CB, who had worked for him loyally before and after the Mutiny of 1857, mentioned once, how, during a drought in Stoke Rowe, his home town, a little boy was beaten by his mother for drinking the last glass of water in the house. Deeply touched by the story, the Maharaja endowed a charity in the form of a free public well in Stoke Rowe. Mr Reade accepted the generous gift and designed the well himself with an Indian style and elegance. Construction, costing £410 18s 1d, began in 1863 on the wedding day of the Prince of Wales, and a year later, in 1864, it was officially opened on Queen Victoria's birthday. It yielded 600–700 gallons of water daily, restricted for cooking and drinking only. During Queen Elizabeth II's visit to India in 1961, the then Maharaja of Banaras presented her with an ivory model of the well and invited Prince Philip to grace the centenary by visiting Stoke Row in 1964. The Prince duly visited the well, taking with him the ivory model, and the ceremony also included the mixing of water from the well with water from the Ganges, specially flown in from India for the occasion.

The interior of Elveden Hall, Suffolk.

The Maharaja's Well at Stoke Row, Henley-on-Thames, Oxfordshire.

To outdo the Maharaja of Banaras, the Maharaja of Vijianagram funded a public **drinking fountain near Marble Arch** in London, and managed to trump the Maharaja of Banaras by inviting royalty, HRH the Duke of Cambridge, to inaugurate it in 1867.

Drinking fountain in Regents Park, London was donated by Sir Cowasji Jehangir CSI (1812–78), a wealthy industrialist from Bombay, in 1869. The ornate and attractive fountain was unveiled by The Princess Mary, Duchess of Teck (1867–1953), who later became Queen Mary. The inscription reads, *This fountain was erected by the Metropolitan Drinking Fountain and Cattle Trough Association, and was the gift of Sir Cowasji Jehangir (Companion of the Star of India), a wealthy Parsee gentleman from Bombay as a token of gratitude to the people of England for the protection enjoyed by him and his fellow countrymen under the British Rule in India.* Inaugurated by HRH Princess Mary, Duchess of Teck, 1869.

Sir Cowasji Jehangir was also present at the opening of the Imperial Institute on 1893 and made a most generous donation of £13,000 and £15,000 on condition that the monies be used for the benefit of the Indian section only. The Governing body of the Institute decided to use the money for the completion of the Indian Conference Room and the Eastern Hall, the lecture theatre.

Maharaja Cooch Behar Fountain in Bexhill-on-Sea, made from marble stone, was inaugurated by Maharaja Jitendra along with the Maharani Indira in 1917, in the presence of the Mayor of Bexhill, Daniel Mayer and Mrs. Mayer. After the ceremony, the Maharaja presented a gold cigarette case and matchbox to the official of the Town Hall. For reasons not known, the Fountain was demolished in 1963.

Above: Plaque to commemorate the lost drinking fountain near Marble Arch.
Far left: The Jehangir Fountain in London's Regents Park.
Left: Maharaja Cooch Behar Memorial Fountain in Bexhill-on-Sea

The Rashtrapati Bhavan in New Delhi, designed by Edwin Lutyens.

Rashtrapati Bhavan – Formerly the Viceroy's Palace in New Delhi. Soon after the King Emperor's Delhi Durbar in 1911, where he declared the transfer of the capital of India from Calcutta to New Delhi, Edwin Lutyens, the architect, was commissioned to design the layout of the new capital. It was the wish of the King that the buildings should be in the Moghul style. On 22nd January 1914, he wrote a letter to the Viceroy, Lord Hardinge saying, 'I hope you will not allow anything to be done "on the cheap". For New Delhi will stand for all time as a monument of British art and workmanship and my name will always be incentivised with it'. It cost ten and a half million pounds and 18 years to complete. Lutyens had asked his friend Sir Herbert Baker, the architect, who later built the India House in London, to collaborate with him to design the Secretariat and the Parliament building.

The 300 room building and the Moghul Gardens, opened in 1931 became the official residence of the Viceroys until 1947, giving them great prominence as the rulers of India. From 1948 to 1950, Chakravarti Rajagopalachari (1878–1972) became the first Indian to occupy the building as the last Governor-General of free India. On 26th January 1950, Dr. Rajendra Prasad (1884–1963), the first President of the Republic of India, moved into the Viceroy's Palace

Inscription on the Jaipur Column in the Rashtrapati Bhavan by Sir Edwin Lutyens:
'In Thought, Faith
In Word, Wisdom
In Deed, Courage
In Life, Service
So may India be Great'

Victoria Memorial in Calcutta is a prominent architectural landmark and a significant reminder of the Raj. It was built by the Viceroy Lord Curzon after the death of Queen Victoria in 1901, the foundation stone was laid by the Prince of Wales, later King George V in 1906. It includes a library with displays of rare books and artifacts such as Tipu Sultan's dagger, cannon used in the battle of Plassey, postage stamps and western paintings.

Viceroy's Lodge in Simla, the summer capital of British India, was built in 1880 in the Jacobethan style. It was used as the venue for the Simla Conference to discuss plans for Indian self-government in 1945 and the partition in 1947. Now the Institute of Advanced Studies

Doors to the Commons Chamber. The House of Commons Chamber was damaged during the Second World War and rebuilt with materials given by the members of the Commonwealth. Entrance doors to the north of the Chamber were a gift from India and those to the south were donated by Pakistan.

Below left: The Victoria Memorial in Calcutta.

Below: The Winter Palace, Simla.

CHAPTER 26
The Legacy of Indian Scientists

The Royal Society, established in 1660 is an independent scientific academy of Britain and the Commonwealth, dedicated to promoting excellence in science. For the reasons of its history and prestige, to be elected a Fellow is considered a great honour.

There have been 49 Indian Fellows, since the election of the first, Ardaseer Cursetjee in 1841. For the first time in its history, the first Indian President, Sir Venktraman Ramakrishnan was elected in 2015. He had shared the Nobel Prize for chemistry in 2009 and awarded a knighthood in 2012. He follows in the footsteps of Sir Christopher Wren, Samuel Pepys and Sir Isaac Newton. The Indian National Science Academy (INSA), established in 1935 is based on The Royal Academy.

Sir Chandrashekhar Venkat Raman (1888–1970), the first Asian Nobel Laureate in physics, was elected a Fellow of the Royal Society in 1924 and is the only Indian to have resigned from the Society. This was because his paper, describing new findings on the physiology of the human eye, was rejected in 1968 with uncomplimentary remarks. Raman was deeply offended and sent a letter of resignation after 44 years of Fellowship.

Venktraman Ramakrishnan.

Table 1. Indian Fellows of the Royal Society, London (1841–2018)

No	Elected	Name	Profession
1	1841	Cursetjee (Wadia), Ardaseer (1808–77)	Shipbuilder, engineer
2	1918	Ramanujan, Srinivasa (1887–1920)	Mathematician
3	1920	Bose, Sir Jagadish Chandra (1858–1937)	Biophysicist
4	1924	Raman, Sir Chandrasekhar Venkat (1888–1970) (w/d 4 April 1968)	Physicist
5	1927	Saha, Meghnad (1893–1956)	Physicist
6	1936	Sahni, Birbal (1891–1949)	Palaeobotanist
7	1940	Krishnan, Sir Kariamanikkam (Srinivasa) (1898–1961)	Physicist
8	1941	Bhabha, Homi Jahangir (1909–1966)	Physicist
9	1943	Bhatnagar, Sir Shanti Swaroop (1895–1955)	Chemist
10	1944	Chandrasekhar, Subrahmanyan (1910–1995)	Astrophysicist
11	1945	Mahalanobis, Prasanta Chander (1893–1972)	Statistician
12	1957	Wadia, Darashaw Nosherwan (1883–1969)	Geologist
13	1958	Bose, Satyendra Nath (1894–1974)	Statistician

Table 1. Indian Fellows of the Royal Society, London (1841–2015), continued

14	1958	Mitra, Sisir Kumar (1890–1963)	Upper-atmosphere physicist
15	1960	Seshadri, Tiruvenkata Rajendra (1900–1975)	Chemist
16	1965	Maheshwari, Panchanan (1904–1966)	Botanist
17	1967	Rao, Calyampudi Radhakrishna (1920–)	Statistician
18	1970	Menon, Mambillikalathil Govind Kumar (1928–)	Physicist
19	1972	Pal, Benjamin Peary (1906–1989)	Agriculturist
20	1973	Harish-Chandra (1923–1983)	Mathematician
21	1973	Swaminathan, Mokombu S. (1925–)	Agriculturist
22	1977	Ramachandran, Gopalasamundram Narayana (1922–2001)	Biophysicist
23	1979	Lal, Devendra (1929–2012)	Physicist
24	1981	Paintal, Autar Singh (1925–2004)	Physiologist
25	1982	Rao, Chintamani Nagesa Ramachandra (1934–)	Chemist
26	1983	Chandrasekhar, Sivaramakrishna (1930–2004)	Crystallographer
27	1984	Siddiqui, Obaid (1932–2013)	Molecular biologist
28	1986	Ramalingaswamy, Vulimiri (1921–2001)	Medical scientist
29	1987	Gopalan, Coluthar (1918–)	Nutritionist
30	1988	Mitra, Ashesh Prasad (1927–2007)	Ionospheric scientist
31	1988	Seshadri, Conjeevaram (1932–)	Mathematician
32	1990	Sharma Man Mohan (1937–)	Chemical engineer
33	1991	Swarup, Govind (1929–)	Radioastronomer
34	1992	Narasimha, Roddam (1933–)	Fluid mechanicist/aeronautist
35	1995	Gurdev Singh Khush (1935–)	Rice breeder
36	1998	Mashelkar, Raghunath Anant (1943–)	Polymer engineer
37	1998	Sen, Ashoke (1956–)	Physicist
38	2000	Raghunathan, Madabusi Santanam (1941–)	Mathematician
39	2000	Ramakrishnan, Tiruppattur Venkatachalamurti (1941–)	Physicist
40	2005	Mehta, Goverdhan (1943–)	Chemist
41	2006	Narayan, Ramesh (1950–)	Astrophysicist
42	2006	Sur, Mriganka (1953–)	Neuroscientist
43	2012	Khare, Chandrashekhar Bhalchandra (1968–)	Mathematician
44	2012	Vidyasagar, Mathukumalli (1947–)	Control theorist
45	2012	Raghavan, Krishaswamy Vijay (1954–)	Geneticist
46	2015	Bawa, Kamal (1939–)	Ecologist
47	2015	Sood, Ajay (1951–)	Physicist
48	2016	Dame Pratibha Gai (1948–)	Electron microscopist
49	2018	Lalita Ramakrishnan (1959–)	Immunologist

CHAPTER 27
Chronology of Events

BC

3500–2500	Indus Valley Civilisation
1500–100	Age of Ramayana, Mahabharata and *Gita*.
563–483	Birth and death of Buddha.
540–468	Birth and Death of Mahavira.
327–325	Alexander the Great in India.
273–232	Reign of Ashoka.

AD

735	First Parsee Settlement from Persia
1000–1026	Muslim invasion of India by Mahmud of Ghazni.
1469	Birth of Guru Nanak.
1498	Vasco de Gama reached Calicut from Portugal.
1510	Portuguese captured Goa.
1526	First Battle of Panipat and establishment of the Moghul Empire by Babur.

1600

1600	East India Company founded by Royal Charter granted by Queen Elizabeth I.
1612	First English factory at Surat.
1614	Sir Thomas Roe appointed England's first envoy to India by King James I. Arrival of an Indian to England officially recorded for the first time.
1616	Sir Thomas Roe appears before Moghul Emperor Jahangir at his Court in Ajmer. The young Indian is baptised at a church in the City of London.
1644	*Farman* (permission) given to the English to trade in Bengal.

1668	First French factory at Surat. Bombay leased to the Company as a most suitable harbour.
1680	East India Company establishes trading centre at Calcutta.
1690	Calcutta established as the third Residency for the Company.
1696	Fort William built in Calcutta, the most impregnable of the Company's buildings in India.
1698	The English obtained Jamindari of the three villages of Sutanati, Kalikata and Gobindapur – nucleus of Calcutta.

1700

1757	Battle of of Plassey. Beginning of the British rule in India.
1765	Robert Clive becomes Governor of Bengal.
1772	Warren Hastings appointed Governor-General of Bengal.
1780	Ranjit Singh establishes Sikh Empire.
1780	First Newspaper, Hickey's *Calcutta Gazette* in India.
1784	Pitt's India Bill passed by Parliament leaves the Company intact but subject to supervision of the Board of Control.
1785	Warren Hastings returns to England.
1799	Death of Tipu Sultan.

1800

1800	Fort William College opened in the new Government House.
1829	Brahmo Samaj founded by Raja Ram Mohan Roy. Abolition of *suttee*.

1835	Introduction of English as the medium of instruction.
1839	Death of Maharaja Ranjit Singh.
1843	Sindh is conquered by Sir Charles Napier and annexed.
1853	Opening of railways and telegraphs.
1854	First postage stamp issued.
1857	Indian Mutiny. Fall of the Moghul dynasty. Bahadur Shah II, the last Moghul Emperor, exiled to Burma where he died in 1862.
1858	Transfer of Indian administration from the East India Company to British Crown.
1860	Lord Macaulay's Indian Penal Code enacted.
1863	Simla, the hill station, becomes the summer seat of government.
1869	Opening of the Suez Canal reduces the journey time from Britain to India from three months to three weeks.
1877	Queen Victoria proclaimed Empress of India
1883	The Ilbert Bill introduced to allow Indian judges and magistrates the jurisdiction to try British offenders in criminal cases, strongly opposed in Britain.
1885	First session of the Indian National Congress in Bombay.

1900

1905	Partition of Bengal by Lord Curzon .
1906	Foundation of the Muslim League.
1911	King George V and Queen Mary atttend the Durbar in New Delhi. Capital of India moves from Calcutta to New Delhi.
1914	Beginning of World War I
1916	Home Rule League founded by Annie Besant.
1918	End of First World War.
1919	Jallianwalla Bagh massacre at Amritsar. Government of India Act.

1928	Simon Commission sent to India to negotiate with Indian politicians to organise a Central government.
1930	First Round Table Conference in London and Gandhi's Salt March to Dandi.
1931	Second Round Table Conference in London. Gandhi and delegates take tea with King George V at Buckingham Palace. Inauguration of New Delhi which took almost twenty years to build.
1932	India play first international cricket match at Lords against England. Military Academy opened at Dehra Dun to train Indians officers instead of going to the Royal Military College, Sandhurst.
1935	Government of India Act introduced to ensure that no single religious group outside Congress dominates the government.
1937	Burma Separated from India.
1939	Second World War declared by the Viceroy Lord Linlithgow without consulting any of the Indian national leaders.
1942	Cripp's Mission to India. 'Quit India' movement in India. Subhash Chandra Bose flees the country and goes to Japan to recruit Indian National Army.
1943	Famine in Bengal, millions starve.
1945	Labour Party comes to power and PM Clement Attlee prepares for Indian independence. WWII ends.
1946	Parliamentary Delegation sent to India to plan for an interim Government.
1947	Lord Mountbatten appointed as the last Viceroy of India. The Congress resigned to the partition and formation of a separate country Pakistan. Nehru becomes the first Prime Minister of the new Dominion of India. Pakistan also becomes a Dominion and Jinnah becomes the Governor-General.
1950	India becomes a Republic on 26 January but remains within the Commonwealth.

Acknowledgements

What started as a small brochure to mark the 400th Anniversary of Indo-British shared heritage has turned into a book. It was inevitable. It was important. Just about every interaction between the peoples of India and of England over the past 400 years has a thread of importance and an element of being historically first. Choosing a significant event or an influential individual that changed the course of history of the two countries was not easy, and yet justice had to be done to every incident that changed lives and every personality that dictated the relationship between India and Britain, good or bad. What has emerged is a very personal look at history and its significance in our everyday lives, swayed by a variety of circumstances both in India and in Britain. It has been an absolute thrill and a pleasure to work on this book.

To Dr Alice Prochaska, Principal of Somerville College, Oxford and Patron, Indo-British Heritage Trust, I extend my most grateful thanks for her Foreword. It has been an honour and a privilege to have her support and the benefit of her experience of working with students from India and Britain to write about the relationship between the two countries. Most importantly, it is to her credit and great personal efforts to go to India to get support to establish the Somerville College Cornelia Sorabji Scholarship for post-graduate law students from India. Her valued contribution is most appreciated.

My most sincere gratitude to Zerbanoo Gifford, Founding Director of the ASHA Centre, for her Foreword and enthusiastic support for all my projects. While I have been looking back at the combined histories of India and Britain, she has brought us up to date, looking at the future of the relationship between the peoples of the two countries and the way forward.

The late Elwyn Blacker, my mentor and friend for over 35 years, was the mastermind behind Project 400. The endless hours he spent researching and laying out the details for the celebration of the historic anniversary formed the blueprint for the programme of events for 2014. Everything that is said and done in the name of this very important project carries the spirit and wisdom of Elwyn Blacker. He would be delighted to know that his sons, Simon and Michael, have taken over where he left off, and with the same degree of interest and commitment. Their encouraging and enthusiastic support has given me great comfort and confidence to carry on with the programme as envisaged by their father.

Project 400 was personally welcomed by the former Prime Minister, the Rt Hon David Cameron MP:

'The 400th anniversary of the arrival of the first Indian in Britain and the appointment of the first British envoy to India will be an opportunity to celebrate our relationship and the contribution of a million and a half British Indians to British society. I have asked the Foreign and Commonwealth Office officials to meet you in order to discuss how we might mark the anniversary together.'

Personal support also came from the Rt Hon Hugo Swire MP, Minister of State: *'As the Prime Minister has stated, we should begin to think about marking this important anniversary. I also hope we can use this opportunity to further underline the importance of the Indian diaspora here in the UK and the benefits these communities bring to the relationship'.*

It is thanks to all the curators, the archivists and the librarians of the various institutions that the gathering of information for the book was made easy. Their kindness and attentiveness is as praiseworthy as it is remarkable. The British Library, the centre for all knowledge, has been the main source of material. My grateful thanks to each and every one who helped, promptly and with utmost courtesy, not only at the desk but also in replying to my letters of enquiry. I am most grateful to Hazel Forsyth, Senior Curator, Medieval and Post-Medieval Collections at the Museum of London, for information in detail about the baptism of the young

Indian in 1616 in the City of London. My grateful thanks to Simon Carter, Collections Manager of St Paul's Cathedral, for the remarkable photographs of the memorials of Indian soldiers, but especially those of the rarely acknowledged WACI 1942–4, the Women's Auxiliary Corps India. Joseph Wisdon, the Librarian of the Chapter House, St Paul's Churchyard, has been most kind in sending me the inscriptions of these memorials.

Richard Dabb of the National Army Museum has been most kind in sending the images of the stained glass windows of the Indian soldiers in the First World War at the Royal Military Academy, Sandhurst. My thanks to him and to Dr A R Morton, Curator at the Academy, for the photograph of the gun used during the battle against Tipu Sultan.

I am particularly grateful to Malcolm Hay, Curator, for the history of the mural in St Stephen's Hall at the Houses of Parliament of Sir Thomas Roe at the Court of the Moghul Emperor Jahangir at Ajmer.

My thanks also to Murray Craig, Clerk to the Chamberlain's Court, Guild Hall, London, for providing the names of early Indian recipients of the Freedom of the City of London. He is the 37th Clerk to the Court since 1294 to admit people to the Freedom of the City of London.

My thanks to Valerie Hart of the City of London Guildhall Library, and to Wendy Hawke, Senior Archivist at the City of London, London Metropolitan Archives, for historic details about the baptism of the young Indian in the City of London in 1616, which have been most valuable. My thanks to Julia Buckley, Archivist at the Royal Botanic Gardens, Kew, and Colnaghi and Niall Hobhouse, Publishers, for their permission to reproduce the drawings of Marianne North and those commissioned by the East India Company.

My most sincere thanks to Professor Anthony Dayan for his chapter on Indo-British scientists, I am deeply touched by his interest and kindness. It has been an honour and a privilege to have his valuable contribution, volunteered with great enthusiasm. To Jeremy Berkhoff my most sincere thanks for his contribution on the history of irrigation and canals in India, and the fascinating piece on his grandfather's life in India. For a computer illiterate, the assistance given by Steve Etter of the ASHA Centre has been a godsend. A computer buff, he has searched out and supplied information from the internet with speed and efficiency and, more importantly, with good humour. My thanks to Graham Coster for his editorial expertise and advice. As for Louise Taylor, who typed the manuscript and checked my final draft, all one can say is that she is an absolute wizard at speed and accuracy. I am most fortunate to have her help, and thank her most sincerely for her kindness and professionalism.

My most grateful thanks to Michele Cornish, who continually looked out for information and publications that could be used for the book. Some of her 'finds' have been most valuable, and are happily included in the book, especially the Blue Plaque in Scotland to Sir John Login.

I am most grateful to Kishore Vadgama for giving me books on British activities in India. *The Great Hedge of India*, about which very little is known, has been as useful as it has been revealing. I owe a great debt of gratitude to Vinoo Sachania for all his help and especially for the photograph of the paving stone memorial to Khudadad Khan. His ever ready help is most appreciated.

To Shrabani Basu, journalist, historian and Founder and Chair of Noor Inayat Khan Memorial Trust, my sincere thanks for her generous contribution on Noor Inayat Khan.

Very special and grateful thanks to Jenny Rowe, Chief Executive, and Ben Wilson, Head of Communications, of the United Kingdom Supreme Court for hosting a debate in 2014 organised by the Indo-British Heritage Trust. Thanks to the Supreme Court as well for permission to mount an exhibition tracing the history of the Indo-British relationship from the Moghul Emperor Akbar the Great and Queen Elizabeth I to then President Pranab Mukherjee and Queen Elizabeth II. It was both an honour and a privilege to be part of their own programme of events marking the role of the Judicial Committee of the Privy Council in the development of common law and related issues across what was the British Empire. Their hospitality, and their invitation to share their own exhibition space honouring, among others, Syed Amir Ali, the first Indian and first Muslim Judge on the Judicial Committee of the Privy Council, are appreciated with gratitude.

I am most grateful to Andy Merriman, author and script writer for his help when ever asked. He has been most kind in giving me ideas and information in relation to my work. His responses have always been prompt and professional over the years. The man is as generous as he is a genius. I have no words to express my gratitude to photographer Rasik Varsani, an ever ready man if ever there was one. At very short notice, he photographed the plaques of the Maharajas of Cooch Behar and the Birla statue. Within an hour of my request, they were done and delivered with courtesy and enthusiasm.

My very special thanks to the Area Manager of Golders Green Crematorium Ms Viv Lackey and in particular Ms Jean Tucker of the Memorial Department for their permission to take photographs of the Maharaja Cooch Behar plaques and the Birla statue. Their kindness is most appreciated.

Patricia Betts, a journalist, has been passing on to me 'all things Indian history' she comes across at her various press meetings. She brought the the most fascinating book about the botanical drawings from India. Two of these unusual paintings from the book are reproduced here, with great delight. A big thanks to her for that and all the other items she has presented to me over the years.

My very special thanks to Ms Jenny Williams, official at the Royal Society, for providing the names of the Indian Fellows of the Society at such short notice.

It is with delight and gratitude that I acknowledge the expert contribution from Anne-Marie Benson for her essay on textiles, she has done me a great honour.

I am most grateful to Dr Umakanth Panchagnula, an anaesthetist by profession with a keen interest in the history of Indian royal families, for giving me the information and photograph of the fountain at Bexhill-on-Sea donated by the Maharaja of Cooch Behar.

My sincere thanks to John Fasal, an Indophile and expert on Indian nobility and Rolls-Royces; for his article and photographs.

I am most grateful to Prof Pankaj Vadgama for his current appraisal of Indo-British collaboration in the field of medical science.

It was a great surprise to receive the photograph of the plaque of Jind Kaur, Maharani of Punjab, from George Hiner and Preeya Vadgama which is published with delight and grateful thanks, also for providing the images of Princess Sophia and Lolita Roy in Parliament Square.

I am extremely grateful to pharmacist and friend Bhasker Thankey and his son Sunit, for all their help.

My very special thanks to Rohin Shah for the picture of Sir William Jones, from his copy of the first volume of Asiatic Society Researches, (1799).

And finally, and very importantly, my thanks to Simon Blacker who has designed the book and Michael Blacker who has helped with production. As well as being brilliant at their creative art, they also have the patience of saints to put up with my endless requests for changes to the text and illustrations. Therefore my heartfelt apologies to them. Either way, I am extremely grateful to have their expertise as well as tolerance, proof enough that the Indo-British relationship can and does survive under any circumstances.

The author

Kusoom Vadgama, Doctor of Optometry, founded the Indo-British Heritage Trust in 2012 and Co-Chairs it with Michael Blacker, with Simon Blacker as an advisor. The year 2014 was the 400th anniversary of the first recorded arrival of an young Indian man to England as well as the appointment, by King James I, of the first English envoy to the Moghul Court in India. In 2014 the Trust inaugurated a debate in the Supreme Court and produced an exhibition to mark the historic events of 400 years of combined history of India and Britain (See YouTube/Empire Debate).

The much neglected history of India in Britain, especially the contributions of the Indian soldiers in the two world wars and the Indo-British relations over the centuries are subjects of special interest to Kusoom. She feels privileged to have been able to, organise, with *India Weekly*, the Centenary celebration of the Indian National Congress with a Gala Dinner in London in 1985; Chair the short-lived Centre for Research in Asian Migration at University of Warwick in 1989; arrange a special event at the Honourable Society of The Inner Temple in 1991 to mark the centenary of Mohandas Karamchand Gandhi being called to the Bar and Chair a special Centenary Dinner in 1992 at the House of Commons to celebrate the election of Dadabhai Naoroji, the first Indian Member of Parliament at Westminster. Kusoom is a Trustee and Treasurer of the Noor Inayat Khan Memorial Trust. In 2011, she was presented with the *Asian Voice* Editor's Award for Research by C B Patel, Editor of the first Asian weekly in Europe.

Other titles by the author

India in Britain 1852–1947 with forewords by Prince Charles and Mrs Indira Gandhi (1984); *India – Indo-British Campaigns in Britain for Indian reforms, justice and freedom*, with a foreword by Dr L M Singhvi (1997); *An Indian Portia – Selected letters of Cornelia Sorabji* (1866–1954) with forewords by Lady Hale of Richmond QC, President of the Supreme Court and Britain's most senior female judge and Coomi Kapoor, Former President, Indian Women's Press Corps (2011).

Index

Bibliography

A Vision of Eden – The Life and Work of Marianne North; Webb and Bower (Publishers) Ltd, London, 1980

Asiatic Researches; or Transactions of the Society, Instituted in Bengal for Enquiring into the History and Antiquities, the Arts, Sciences, and Literature of Asia, London, 1799.

Basu, Shrabani, Spy Princess; Sutton Publishing, Stroud, 2006

Berkoff, Jeremy, Who Do I think I Am?; London, 2014

Brown, Michael J, Itinerant Ambassador; University Press of Kentucky, Lexington, 1970

Calcutta Review, Volume 13, 1924

Chatterji, Usha and Zaneta, Jean-Gabriel, Stamps and History of the Republic of India; Oliver Perrin, 1975

Crystal, David (edited), Cambridge Encyclopaedia; Cambridge University Press, Cambridge, 1993

Cummings, Debra, Acting With Intent: How Queen Victoria brought India home to Britain through an Indian prince and an Indian servant. Graduate Annual, Vol II, La Salle University, 2014.

De Maré, Eric, The Year of the Great Exhibition; The Folio Press, J M Dent Ltd, London, 1973

Edwards, Michael, The Battle of Plassey; B T Batsford Ltd, London, 1963

Fifty-One Flowers; Colnaghi, London, 2006

Forbes, Geraldine, Women of Colonial India; Chronicle Books, New Delhi, 2005

Forsyth, Hazel, The Cheapside Hoard: London's Lost Jewels; Philip Wilson Publishers, London, 2013

Gibbs-Smith, C H, The Great Exhibition of 1851, London; His Majesty's Stationery Office, 1950;

Commemorative Album, compiled by C H Gibbs-Smith

Guy, Alan J & Boyden, Peter B, Soldiers of the Raj: The Indian Army 1600–1947; National Army Museum, 1997

Hood, Jean, Trafalgar Square; B T Batsford, London, 2005

I'tesamuddin Mirza Sheikh, The Wonders of Vilayet; translated by Kaiser Haq; Peepal Tree Press Ltd, Leeds, 2001

Jones, Jonathan, The Guardian; London, 2003

Keay, John, India – A History; HarperCollins, London, 2000

Mahajan, V D, India Since 1526; S Chand and Company, 1991

Mee, Arthur, London the Great City Complete; Hodder & Stoughton Ltd, 1948

Mehrotra, S R, Times of India; 31 July, 1988

Misra Jaishree, Rani; Penguin Books India, 2007

Moorehouse, Geoffrey, India Britannica; Harvill Press, London, 1983

Moulton, Edward, C, Ahead of His Time and Still Relevant: A O Hume's Administrative Initiatives and Philosophical Ideas; 2012

Moulton, Edward C, Early Indian Nationalism: Henry Cotton and the British Positivist and Radical Connection 1870–1950

Moxham, Roy, The Great Hedge of India; Constable, London, 2001

O'Connor, Daniel, The Chaplains of the East India Company 1601–1848; Continuum, 2011

Paxman, Jeremy, Empire; Viking, London, 2011

Queen Mary's Book for India; Harrap, London, 1943

Rao, G. Subba, Indian Words in English; Oxford, 1954

Robertson, Alan, Epic Engineering – Great Canals and Barrages in Victorian India; edited and completed by Jeremy Berkoff; Beechwood Melrose Publishing, 2013

Robinson, Francis, The Moghul Emperors; Thames & Hudson, London, 2007

Sastri Srinivasa, Rt Hon, The Life and Times of Sir Pheroze Shah Mehta; Bharatiya Vidya Bhavan, 1975

Sen, Keshub Chunder, Keshub Chunder Sen in England – A Writers' Workshop; Greyhound Book, 1870

Strachan, Michael, Sir Thomas Roe (1581–1644): A Life; Michael Russell Publishers

Sumeray, Derek and Sheppard, John, London Plaques; Shire Publications, 1999

The Dictionary of National Biography; Oxford University Press, Oxford, 1992

The Great Exhibition of 1851: Descriptive and Illustrated Catalogue, Part IV – Colonies and Foreign States Division I

The History of Modern Cremation in Great Britain from 1874; The Cremation Society of Great Britain, Kent

The Indian Army – Soldiers of the Raj 1600–1947, Edited by Alan Jay Guy and Peter B Boydon; National Army Museum, 1997.

The Raj – India and the British 1600–1947; National Portrait Gallery Publications, 1990

The Times Book of India; Times Publishing Co Ltd, 1930

Vadgama, Kusoom, An Indian Portia – Selected Letters of Cornelia Sorabji 1866–1954; Blacker Ltd, 2011

Vadgama, Kusoom, India – British-Indian Campaigns in Britain for Indian Reforms, Justice & Freedom 1831–1947; Banyan Tree Publishing, London, 1997

Vadgama Kusoom, India in Britain; Robert Royce, 1984

Wikipedia: the Free Encyclopaedia

Williamson, Laureen D, The Illustrated History of the Maharaja's Well; Maharaja's Well Trust, Stock Row, 1983.

Photographic Credits

All images are from the Author's private collection or from royalty-free sources unless stated.

15 (br)	Courtesy of the Marquis of Salisbury
19 (bl)	Courtesy National Portrait Gallery
20	Courtesy National Portrait Gallery
23	Courtesy Shropshire Council Museums (SHYAMS: FA/ 1990/36)
25	Brighton & Hove Museum
30	Courtesy National Portrait Gallery
32	© Sandhurst Collection
38	Courtesy of the Walters Art Museum
40	Simon Blacker
45	Johan Joseph Zoffany RA, *Warren Hastings,* Yale Center for British Art, Paul Mellon Fund
53	Courtesy National Portrait Gallery
57	Courtesy of Colnaghi
58	Floral paintings by Marianne North, © RBG Kew
68	© British Library Board (WD 1012)
70	Courtesy Jeremy Berkoff
77 (b)	Courtesy Peeple Tree Press Ltd
78 (bl)	Brighton & Hove Museum
78 (br)	Brighton & Hove Museum
100	© International Atomic Energy Agency
106	NASA – Kalpana Chawla
109 (bl)	www.bollywoodhungama.com
110 (c)	www.bollywoodhungama.com
112	Courtesy of National Gallery Modern Art, Delhi
125	© National Army Museum
137	© British Library Board (Photo 13/1)
169	© Sandhurst Collection
170 (tl, tr)	Courtesy of Chapter of St Paul's Cathedral
171 (t)	Courtesy St Luke's Church
174 (c)	Courtesy Umakanth Panchagnula

Front cover montage, clockwise from top left: Dr Rajendra Prasad, the first President of Independent India; Taj Mahal, Agra; William Carey, English Baptist missionary, 1793; Statue of Laxmibai, the Rani of of Jhansi and her adopted son; Queen Victoria, Empress of India; Bronze tiger memorial to Tipu Sultan of Mysore; Emperor Shah Jahan, detail from *Jujhar Singh Bundela Kneels in Submission to Shah Jaha*n, *c.*1630.
Back cover: Dadabhai Naoroji, the first Indian MP at Westminster 1892; The Royal Pavilion, Brighton.